THE CATHOLIC SHRINES OF EUROPE

THE CATHOLIC SHRINES of EUROPE

Gerard E. Sherry

Our Sunday Visitor Publishing Division
Our Sunday Visitor, Inc.
Huntington, Indiana 46750

International Standard Book Number: 0-87973-548-1
Library of Congress Catalog Card Number: 86-62664

Cover design by James E. McIlrath

PRINTED IN THE UNITED STATES OF AMERICA

548

Acknowledgments

Scripture texts appearing in this book
are taken from the *Revised Standard Version Bible,
Catholic Edition,* © 1965 and 1966
by the Division of Christian Education
of the National Council
of the Churches of Christ in the U.S.A.,
and used by permission of the copyright owner.
If any copyrighted materials
have been inadvertently used in this book
without proper credit being given,
please notify Our Sunday Visitor in writing
so that future printings of this work
may be corrected accordingly.

Contents

Foreword > On Pilgrimage < 11

1 > Walsingham < 15

2 > Canterbury < 27

3 > Glastonbury < 38

4 > Santiago de Compostela < 49

5 > Our Lady of the Pillar < 59

6 > Lourdes < 68

7 > Miraculous Medal Shrine < 81

8 > Our Lady of Fátima < 91

9 > Częstochowa < 103

10 > St. Meinrad of Einsiedeln < 112

MAP SHOWING LOCATION OF SHRINES ON PAGE 9

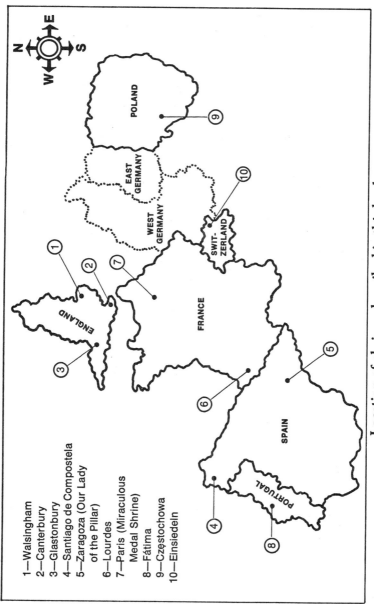

1—Walsingham
2—Canterbury
3—Glastonbury
4—Santiago de Compostela
5—Zaragoza (Our Lady
    of the Pillar)
6—Lourdes
7—Paris (Miraculous
    Medal Shrine)
8—Fátima
9—Częstochowa
10—Einsiedeln

Location of shrines described in this book

On Pilgrimage

Through Scripture and through participation in the liturgy we have come to realize that we are a pilgrim Church and a pilgrim people. Every day of our lives we travel that much nearer to God, wittingly or unwittingly, conscious of that fact or perhaps even resisting it. We are always on pilgrimage either spiritually or physically.

The Old Testament is replete with examples of religious gatherings at particular sanctuaries. For example, Jerusalem became the focal point for Israelites after King David brought the Ark of the Covenant to the city.

In the New Testament, we have the beautiful story of the boy Jesus in the Temple. Every year the Holy Family went on pilgrimage to Jerusalem for the Passover. On the return journey, Joseph and Mary had traveled for a day before realizing Jesus was not with the group of pilgrims. When they went back, they found Jesus in the Temple with the Jewish teachers (see Luke 2:41-52). In this Gospel story, we have another proof of the antiquity and meaningfulness of pilgrimages to holy sanctuaries.

Modern pilgrims to the various shrines of the world have it relatively easy compared with their forebears. Transportation today is comfortable, fast, and safe, rather than being wearisome, tedious, and even relatively hazardous. People nowadays suffer primarily from jet lag. But consider the early centuries, when there was hardly any mode of travel other than the donkey, the horse, or one's own two feet. Unless you were very rich or otherwise privileged, your resting place at the end of the day was likely to be open to the sky and the elements. Food was whatever you could carry along with you: a bit of cheese, some dried fruit, and a little wine as protection against unfit water. There was one other truly major problem for these early pilgrims — traveling without guards meant they were exposed to the constant danger of attack by brigands or capture by other types of hostile forces. Being held for ransom or sold into slavery was not an uncommon fate.

It was for this reason that the early rulers in Christian countries, and indeed the popes of those times, felt it necessary and their responsibility to build pilgrim roads and erect places of accommodation. All this was done, along with taking steps to protect the travelers as they passed through each region. As early as the sixth century, Pope St. Symmachus is said to have expressed interest in the safety of pilgrims who journeyed to Rome. The pilgrim road through France to Spain and the shrine of Santiago de Compostela had a number of hospices all along the way, all under the patronage of the various kings.

So too some of the ancient orders of chivalry were originally created expressly to assist needy, sick, and unarmed pilgrims. In addition, confraternities were set up in many countries solely to help pilgrims.

When pilgrims arrived at a shrine, they usually left a gift of money or oil or wax, depending on their means. The oil and wax were an essential part of the illumination of a shrine and aided in its maintenance. Some shrine churches in the Middle Ages depended on such offerings for their survival. Many thrived on them and flourished materially as well as spiritually. Excavations in Rome unearthed seventh-century Anglo-Saxon coins, attesting to the presence of English pilgrims to the tomb of St. Peter. What a long and arduous journey it had to be, one undertaken only with a sense of devotion to the Apostle!

Pilgrims made vows to say prayers and do acts of penance for their sins so that their transgressions would be expiated at the holy places they visited. Many walked the pilgrim roads barefoot and knelt for hours on rough stone at the shrines. The modern pilgrim tends to pray on comfortable kneelers and wear appropriate footwear wherever he goes.

This book is an invitation to go on pilgrimage. We will explore some of the famous shrines of Europe, examine their origins, and consider what they mean to us as a pilgrim Church and a pilgrim people. Some of us will actually take off on the modern pilgrim roads — via the jet streams, the expressways, the German autobahns, the Italian autostradas, and perhaps an occasional mountain pathway. Others may have to stay at home — there are any number of reasons that could prevent us from physically joining a pilgrimage. That doesn't matter at all, for there is the opportunity for each of us to be a pilgrim in spirit, joining in prayer with our fellow members of the people of God who cross the oceans, journeying to Lourdes, Fátima, Walsingham, Częstochowa, Einsiedeln, Glastonbury, Canterbury, Santiago de Compostela, Our Lady of the Pillar Basilica in Zaragoza, and the Shrine of the Miraculous Medal in Paris.

Reading the history of these shrines and understanding their purpose and attraction will get us into the spirit of pilgrimage. From that point we can join in the meditation which invites our prayerful participation, joining our lives with Jesus and Mary as we slowly, and sometimes painfully, wend our way up the pilgrim road to eternity.

And for some, nothing more than an easy chair is needed to get us into that spirit.

— G.E.S.

CHAPTER ONE

Walsingham

The treasured traditions of the Church with which we can enrich our lives include reading about or, if we are very fortunate, traveling to the ancient shrines of Christendom. Built with love and skilled artistry, cathedrals and tiny wayside chapels alike reflect the faith and devotion of those inspired to create them. That inspiration took many forms, and the stories of what motivated people are handed down to us in legends, poems, and even song.

Visions are almost always the origin of shrines to Mary, the Mother of God. In modern times we have come to accept without hesitation appearances of Our Lady at Fátima, Lourdes, Guadalupe, and a host of other places in Europe, South America, and Asia. Remarkable too has been the fact Mary seldom has been reported as appearing to anyone but simple, faith-filled people — and always in a quiet countryside setting. The story of Walsingham, though ancient, will start us off on this pilgrimage.

Centuries before the celebrated Marian shrines that we know today were established, England had the reputation of being "the Dowry of Mary." It was a well-earned reputation, for its countryside was dotted with shrines to the Blessed Mother. Extraordinary devotion to her can be traced back to the earliest foundation of Christianity in the British Isles. Long before the Norman Conquest (1066), pilgrims of Our

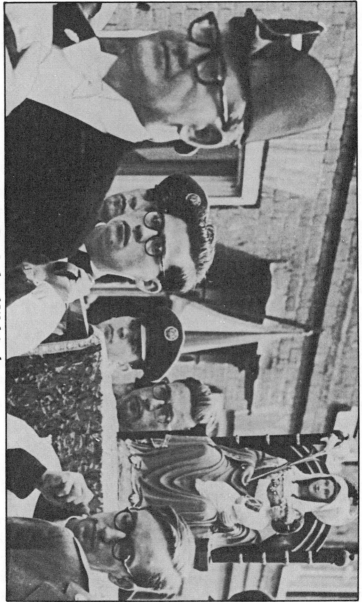

Our Lady of Walsingham

RNS Photo

Lady trudged the sturdy Roman roads that had been built generations before them. Built, in fact, even before Augustine brought the Catholic faith to their country.

Every few miles there were devotional places. Some were large impressive churches, adorned with skillfully carved stone and woodwork; others were simple folk shrines, cruder in their artistic efforts but inspired equally by love of God. All catered to the perennial pilgrims who sought spiritual and material comfort through prayer and penitential rites. The most famous of the pre-Reformation shrines was dedicated to Our Lady at Walsingham. Walsingham was an out-of-the-way little hamlet in the east-coast county of Norfolk. A green and pleasant spot, peaceful and close to the sea, it was neither fashionable nor famous. Nevertheless, and despite its location off the beaten track, it grew to preeminence in Saxon times as a place of pilgrimage. When St. Edward the Confessor was king of England and the faith was strong, Walsingham was a treasured place of devotion.

The historic origins of Walsingham are very sketchy, but legend has it that a woman of the village, Richeldis de Faverches, was blessed by a vision in which the Blessed Virgin "led her in spirit" to the Holy Land. There, she was shown the house of the Annunciation, where Mary spoke with the angel Gabriel and consented to become the Mother of God. The Virgin asked the Lady Richeldis to build a similar house in Walsingham and promised to help anyone who sought her intercession.

According to the late H.M. Gillett, noted Catholic historian and expert on Walsingham, Lady Richeldis hastened to fulfill the commission, hiring skilled craftsmen to build the house just as she had seen it in the vision. However, after the house was erected, there was doubt as to whether it was situated on the correct site chosen by Mary. In one of his books on the shrine, Gillett tells of the sequel:

"The difficulty was partly solved, however, by a strange manifestation, which seemed miraculously to indicate Our Lady's wishes. There was a heavy fall of dew which soaked all the surface of the meadow wherein it had been planned to set the shrine, with the exception of two small rectangles of grass, both of which were left equally dry. One of these patches lay near two wells, and it was on this that it was decided to lay the foundations on which the wooden house was to rest. But before the house could be erected, a new difficulty arose. Nothing the workmen could do would make the foundation fit the house, labor as they might. By sunset the task was no nearer completion than in the morning, so that, 'all sorry and sad,' they went home to rest.

"But that night, knowing Our Lady who had first made known her intentions might wish to assist in the matter, Lady Richeldis spent the entire night in prayer. And in answer, with the aid of angels' hands, Our Lady caused the whole house to be lifted up and to be set in the other space 200 feet or more away. Next morning when the craftsmen came to complete their unfinished work, they found the house was already set up, and that with a workmanship far superior to their own. Thus it was the outcome of a vision, and the work of angels' hands, the new Nazareth, England's most celebrated shrine prior to the Reformation, was set up in a remote corner of Norfolk."

The growth and influence of the Walsingham shrine was phenomenal. Local families gave grants of land to enlarge the area and to house the increasing number of pilgrims. Trade in the town grew, and the people flourished both spiritually and materially. In 1153, the Augustinian Canons established a priory, with an eventual huge church; but the Holy House still remained the center of the major devotion.

Henry III is said to have been the first king of England to visit the shrine as a pilgrim, in 1226. He returned several times and started a trend of royal patronage for Walsingham. For the next three centuries, all the kings and queens of England were frequent visitors, and their influence guaranteed its prestige and importance as an international Marian shrine. Throngs accompanied the royal personages, and crowds visited the shrine following the departure of royalty.

It is recorded in various histories of the time that because of Walsingham's popularity, people from all walks of life made bequests to the shrine in their wills. Although it was in a remote part of England, the shrine became known throughout the land and all over Europe. In fact, it became so well-known and popular that some time in his or her life almost every English person hoped to visit the shrine. And significantly, the Elizabethan chronicler Holinshed selected the road to Walsingham as the first among his roads through England. In that era, the four great shrines of Christendom were recorded as Walsingham, Rome, San Diego (Santiago) de Compostela, and Jerusalem. Of all these shrines, Walsingham was the only one dedicated to the Blessed Virgin.

Walsingham thrived until the sixteenth century. The notorious Henry VIII made a pilgrimage to the shrine in 1511, giving thanks for the birth of a son, Prince Henry. The king, it is said, had a great devotion to Our Lady; he had financed the shrine chaplain and paid an annual endowment for the King's Candle burning before the statue of the Madonna of Walsingham. Alas, his refusal of allegiance to the pope, after the Holy See's denial of his request for divorce, set in motion the partial destruction of the Catholic Church in England.

Walsingham became one of the victims of the ecclesiastical terrorism that ensued. The priory was closed, the Augustinians were sent away, and the Holy House was burned to the ground. The statue of Our Lady was taken from Walsingham to London, where it was desecrated. It seemed the end of the shrine and the devotion. For almost three hundred fifty years the town was a sleepy backwater. The priory was in ruins, and no one seemed interested in preserving the memory of the Virgin of Walsingham.

It wasn't until after the Catholic Emancipation Act of 1829, and a period when religious freedom was once again assured in England, that revival of the shrine was initiated. An Anglican woman purchased the fourteenth-century Slipper Chapel, located a mile outside Walsingham, in 1890, and later made a pilgrimage to all the existing Marian shrines of Europe. After the trip, she converted to Roman Catholicism and devoted herself to the restoration of the Walsingham shrine. At the time of this activity, there wasn't one Catholic living in the village and it was part of the parish of Kings Lynn, several miles away. For a number of years, the Kings Lynn parish church was used for commemoration of Walsingham while the original Slipper Chapel remained unused.

One point of interest is the fact that there is a pontifical shrine at Kings Lynn, established after the Catholic Emancipation Act in 1829. The Lady Chapel there is the "Holy House" — a most beautiful structure, endowed with the statue of Our Lady of Walsingham, given in 1897 by Pope Leo XIII as a personal gift to English Catholics. In this same year, the Slipper Chapel was purchased and given back to the Catholic Church. Even during the penal times — from late in the reign of Henry VIII, until the Emancipation Act — Catholics still continued to venerate Our Lady of Walsingham. As a tribute to his role in spreading the devotion to Our Lady of Walsingham, the historian Gillett — who was also the founder of the Ecumenical Society of the Blessed Virgin Mary — has his ashes enclosed in the walls of the Slipper Chapel.

It took almost fifty years after the purchase of the Slipper Chapel for the first Mass since the Reformation to be celebrated within its walls. Soon after, a national pilgrimage led by the then archbishop of Westminster, Cardinal Francis Bourne, went to Walsingham. This act officially restored the shrine and the devotion to the Virgin of Walsingham. Since that time, housing for pilgrims has been erected, and programs of spiritual renewal are an ongoing part of the shrine project.

The ecumenical aspect of Walsingham is very important. The Anglicans have built a magnificent shrine church for their own communicants and it attracts thousands to the area. In addition, there is an annual joint pilgrimage of the adherents of both faiths on the Monday after Pentecost Sunday when prayers for Christian unity are recited.

Of special interest is the bond between America and Walsingham that was established during World War II. Many U.S. servicemen were stationed on the east coast of England; with their chaplains they visited Walsingham, and it became a place of pilgrimage for them too. Some still go back there when they revisit Europe. From this recent tradition, an American shrine to Our Lady of Walsingham has been created in the parish of St. Bede in Williamsburg, Virginia. The main altar of the parish church is fashioned after the original one in Walsingham, and parish devotion to the Walsingham Virgin is a weekly exercise.

Getting to Walsingham from London is easy. There are good motorways to Norwich and Kings Lynn, both twenty-seven miles away. And from both these towns the signs pointing toward the shrine are more than adequate. By rail there is good service to Norwich and Kings Lynn. Buses from these two towns have frequent service to the shrine, especially during the summer months. And if you prefer a bus-coach from London, there is one daily trip that stops at Fakenham, five miles from Walsingham. Then you take a local bus to complete the journey.

Pilgrim accommodations are available in Walsingham and surrounding towns for individuals, families, or large groups. It's not luxury living, but it is clean and comfortable — and at very affordable rates. There are also specialized accommodations for the sick, elderly, and handicapped.

What may one expect at Walsingham? First, there is the Slipper Chapel, which is the English national shrine to Our Lady. There is also the Anglican parish church of St. Mary's, which is the Church of England's Marian shrine. In addition, there is the Roman Catholic parish of the Annunciation, as well as a Methodist chapel and the Greek-Orthodox church of St. Seraphim. There are several religious and lay houses in the area, including those of the Marist Fathers, the Marist Sisters, the Little Sisters of Jesus, the Sons of Divine Providence, the Sisters of St. Margaret (Anglican), and the Knights of Malta.

Other points of interest are Abbey Grounds (site of the original shrine), the ancient pump house, friary ruins, and Shirehall Museum. The area abounds with small hotels sporting medieval names such as the Black Lion, and pubs such as the Robin Hood. And to show the diverse ethnic groups that have settled, even in rural England, there is the Bangkok Restaurant, as well as tea rooms serving the famous British high tea.

A typical day at the shrine has the following schedule:

8:15 A.M. — Morning prayer of the Church at the parish church.

8:45 A.M. — Parish daily Mass.

9:45 A.M. — Procession to the shrine.

10:30 A.M — Confessions at the Chapel of Reconciliation.

Noon — Pilgrim Mass at the Chapel of Reconciliation.

2:30 P.M. — Procession to the village and benediction at the parish church.

3:00-4:00 P.M. — Adoration of the Blessed Sacrament. Time for private devotion followed by benediction at the Chapel of Reconciliation.

4:00-4:30 P.M. — Confessions on request.

4:40 P.M. — Rosary at Slipper Chapel.

5:00 P.M. — Mass at the Chapel of Reconciliation.

6:15 P.M. — Evening prayer at the parish church.

8:00 P.M. — Pilgrim service at the parish church.

This religious activity is held on a daily basis from March to October. During the winter months, it is curtailed except for large groups of visitors. To the Marist Fathers who staff the shrine, the purpose of the restored Walsingham is to continue its ancient ministry to all who seek God. And in stressing Christian unity the Marists echo the hopes of the pilgrims for another great day when there will be one shrine and one pilgrimage.

Not all of us can make the journey to Walsingham, but there is no reason why we cannot be "pilgrims" in spirit and meditate on the meaning of the original shrine — a constant reminder of the incarnation of Christ.

MEDITATION

The beautiful and fervent faith of the builders of Mary's Holy House in Walsingham enabled them to visualize the simple Nazareth home of Mary. The village home was surely a tiny structure serving to provide shelter from both the dangers of darkness and the heat of the day for all those who dwelled within. Unlike the palaces of princes, it was not a place for idle leisure nor was it decorated by artists. Outside were the sounds and noises of country life: children shouting at play, women gossiping as they worked at daily chores, men joking and arguing over prices and problems. On the hillside nearby, the young shepherds stood watch over sheep. In a house built with clay and rock gathered from the hillside lived the young Mary and her parents. She was happily and contentedly betrothed to the village carpenter, Joseph. It was there, shielded by sturdy earthen walls from whatever evils or dangers lay without, that the angel Gabriel spoke to Mary and heard her acceptance of the role God asked her to perform for the salvation of the world.

The Holy House in Walsingham is a sign and a

symbol of that most incredible moment in the history of mankind when the deep faith of a young girl enabled her to comprehend the high calling God offered her, and her love for God gave her the courage to step forth in faith.

The Gospel of Luke (1:26-38) tells us that it was in the unadorned village home that the angel Gabriel promised Mary that her Son would be great, that he would be given the throne of David, and that his kingdom would have no end. It was there that Mary, after a few fearful protests, spoke those vital words heard alike in medieval Walsingham and the modern world: "Behold, I am the handmaid of the Lord; let it be [done] to me according to your word" (Luke 1:38).

CHAPTER TWO

Canterbury

Nearly six centuries ago, the pilgrims in Geoffrey Chaucer's *Canterbury Tales* made their leisurely way through England to the shrine of St. Thomas the Martyr. In the centuries since, pilgrims still journey to the spot where Thomas à Becket, archbishop of Canterbury, was struck down by agents of King Henry II.

The king had been well served over the years by Thomas, and when Thomas was appointed to the see of Canterbury, he was expected to continue to respond favorably to the king's wishes. Instead, Thomas took an independent stand, choosing to serve God first and the king second. The king was reported to have exclaimed in annoyance with Thomas, "Who will rid me of this troublesome priest?" Four knights, taking the king's words literally, went to the cathedral and killed Thomas à Becket. Almost immediately the popular archbishop was hailed as a saint and martyr. Canterbury became a shrine of great significance, attracting pilgrims from Britain and the Continent.

But Canterbury has a history that goes back even beyond December 29, 1170, when St. Thomas was martyred. It was once a sizable Roman city but was abandoned with the fall of the Roman Empire. The Saxons invaded the unprotected city and stayed. Although he was a pagan, the Saxon king Ethelbert — influenced by his Christian queen, Bertha — sent

Canterbury Cathedral

pleas to Rome for missionaries. Missionaries would bring learning, culture, and the stability of the Church's teaching to his kingdom; so it was both a joy and an honor when, in the year of Our Lord 597, forty Benedictine monks arrived. Ethelbert was baptized by the prior Augustine, who was then consecrated archbishop of Canterbury.

During the peaceful Saxon times that followed, a cathedral was begun, enlarged, and enhanced, but all was destroyed by fire in 1067. The Normans rebuilt Canterbury Cathedral on the same site, creating the present great Romanesque building for the use of the Benedictines. This is the cathedral in which Thomas à Becket was murdered. In the latter Middle Ages it was added on to, portions were rebuilt, and impressive towers were constructed in the Gothic style. Whatever was done, St. Thomas's shrine was always the centerpiece for Canterbury and the reason pilgrims came. Reports of miracle healings and other blessings were constantly recorded. The Reformation saw an end to that era of frequent pilgrimages, when Henry VIII caused the shrine to be destroyed. Fortunately, the church building itself was spared in both the upheavals of the Reformation and the bombings of World War II.

The pilgrim visiting Canterbury today can enter under the lofty spans of the cathedral and walk through quiet beauty to the back of the main altar where St. Thomas's shrine was located. Or better yet, the pilgrim can enter the cathedral through Martyrdom Door at the end of the cloister walk and find himself immediately at the spot where the archbishop was murdered. The knights had followed St. Thomas around the cloister and there they caught up with him, committing their heinous crime. Standing in the place where a man laid down his life for principles, one can get the sense of all the centuries that have gone before; and one can almost imagine rubbing shoulders with long-ago pilgrims — both the aristocracy and commoners — who there honored the memory of Thomas the Martyr. The ancient shrine may be gone, but the remembrance of St. Thomas is kept alive in our literature, not only in *The Canterbury Tales*, but in modern theater and in such contempory works as T.S. Eliot's *Murder in the Cathedral*. It was there too that Pope John Paul II and the present archbishop of Canterbury knelt together in prayer.

The Roman Catholic Church changed hands during the Reformation and became a part of the state church, the Church of England. The post-Reformation period brought in a host of Protestant refugees, mostly Huguenots from France. Many settled in Kent, especially around Canterbury, at the invitation of Queen Elizabeth I. She allowed them the use of the cathedral crypt and, according to Anglican Church authorities, they have continued to worship God in French in the crypt right down to the present day. During the time of Elizabeth, Puritanism was gaining ground, and its adherents alleged that the break with the Church of Rome was not enough, that the English reformation was incomplete. They condemned ritual and religious holidays and practiced a rigorous form of morality which saw an occasion of sin in almost every activity in life.

Canterbury Cathedral was one of the targets of Puritan fanatics, who caused great damage to its fabric and priceless stained glass. This happened during the Great Rebellion in the reign of Charles I. It wasn't until 1660, when Charles II was restored to his throne, that Canterbury returned to peace and prosperity. The next big change came during the Victorian era, when the railways spread out from London. Increased prosperity came to the region and produced much building and an expansion of commerce that continued through World War II in the cathedral city.

The years between the two world wars saw changes in the life of Canterbury Cathedral. Interest in the past and particularly in St. Thomas à Becket increased, and the cathedral once more became a center of religious pilgrimage and cultural festivals. London's St. Paul's Cathedral and Westminster Abbey had been the focal points for much of the country's religious life. It was in these two cathedrals that much of the nation's ceremonials had taken place, but the primatial see of the official Anglican Church was still Canterbury, and the Anglican hierarchy were delighted that people were becoming aware of Canterbury Cathedral's history and position.

During World War II, the old city suffered terribly from the German air raids of 1942, but providentially the great cathedral came through the ordeal practically unscathed. The rebuilding of the city, along with the enlargement of its boundaries through the reorganization of municipal government in 1974, has created a much larger population and increased the city's importance in that part of England. Its stature is enhanced by being the home of the University of Kent, Christ Church College, and many cultural and technological institutions. Its spiritual and cultural heritage makes Canterbury a special place when touring England. Going as a pilgrim, not merely as a tourist, enables the visitor to glory in the cathedral's unique Catholic past. Praying at the tombs of martyrs and confessors enriches one's comprehension of the continuity of Christendom.

Getting there is easy from London. There is adequate train and bus service, and the roads into the city are excellent. The new circular highway around London, M25, enables quick access to Kent from any part of London, and the highway to Canterbury is well marked. If you want to go on foot, as did the travelers of old, there is the ancient Pilgrims Way. But be warned! It will take you several days to follow that route. This, of course, is the route that Chaucer and his friends took six hundred years ago. It was also the route taken a hundred years later by the great Christian scholar Erasmus. Significantly, no matter what route you take, no matter what mode of travel, the view on approaching the city will not be too different than that experienced by these earlier pilgrims: You see the great towers of Canterbury Cathedral still dominating the skyline. It's a place where a tourist can become a pilgrim, and where a pilgrim can enjoy being also a tourist.

Accommodations are no problem whatsoever, both in the city and in the surrounding countryside. You can choose modern hotels or ancient inns. If you have already got accommodations in London, you might consider just a day trip. However, be prepared to change your mind once you get there, as you'll probably find that you want to spend more time and seek local bed and breakfast. And if you want just that, there are plenty of private homes that offer it at very reasonable prices. Anyone having difficulties in that regard can always contact the several tourist information offices which are available in most parts of the city.

What to see? There is so much, and all of it is full of Catholic history. On approaching the city from the London Road, there is the old church of St. Dunstan; within it is buried the head of another martyr, St. Thomas More, the lord chancellor of England who chose his God over his king (Henry VIII). When Sir Thomas was beheaded at the Tower of London on July 6, 1535, he died saying that he remained "the king's good servant but God's first." St. Thomas More's daughter, Margaret Roper, once lived in the area and brought her father's head to lie in the Roper family vault.

Like many modern cities, Canterbury has attempted to deal with some of its problems by turning the main street into a pedestrian mall. If you look about you, you will notice that there are still many old houses with tiled roofs modernized only by fronts. On this street also are two beautiful churches. One, the parish church of St. Peter, has a small bell tower that is supposedly of Saxon origin. Take the time to admire its stained glass and a very old baptismal font. The other church is Methodist, with an 1811 façade and original galleries, paneled apse, and tall pulpit. It is an original example of a Nonconformist place of worship in the early nineteenth century.

Another center of attraction is the ruins of Blackfriars, a Dominican friary that dominated one part of Canterbury from its founding in 1237 until its dissolution during the Reformation. The church and cloister were destroyed; only the refectory and guest hall survived, with the latter now beautifully restored. The Franciscan Gardens are another "must site" to visit. This is a strikingly beautiful thirteenth-century home that once belonged to the Grey Friars. The Grey Friars were the first Franciscans to settle in England; they arrived in the country during the lifetime of St. Francis himself.

Other points of interest include the Poor Priests Hospital, founded in the thirteenth century as an almshouse for elderly celibate clergy. It is now the city museum. Next is St. Mildred's Church, which is of Saxon origin. Inside the church are interesting monuments; and, according to the parish register, Izaak Walton married Rachel Fludde there in 1626. Then there is the Old Tower of St. George's Church — it is all that remained of the church (which dated back to the early 1500s) after a German air raid in June of 1942. Christopher Marlowe, Canterbury's famous playwright, was baptized at St. George's on February 26, 1564. There are also two interesting hospital buildings with historical import. The first, St. John the Baptist Hospital, is said to be the oldest almshouse still surviving in England and perhaps even in Europe. It was founded by a friend of William the Conquerer, Archbishop Lanfranc, then abbot of Caen, in 1084. Its service to elderly men and women continues to this day. Jesus' Hospital, also an almshouse, was founded by a wealthy Elizabethan lawyer. Although its purpose was to serve old and needy persons, it also provided a school for indigent boys. The school was maintained by the warden of the hospital for almost three hundred years, until it was merged with others into a grammar school in 1879.

There are many more interesting places and buildings to see, but we had better talk about the main purpose of our Canterbury visit — its famous cathedral. On the way to it, we come across the cloister at the western entrance and discover some new heraldry set amid the medieval. Newly carved and painted are the coats of arms of Pope John Paul II, Archbishop Robert Runcie (primate of the Church of England), and Charles, prince of Wales. They commemorate the meeting of the three on the occasion of John Paul's visit to England, and specifically to Canterbury on May 29, 1982.

The Martyrdom Door of Canterbury Cathedral,

as mentioned earlier, is the spot where Thomas à Becket was assassinated on the evening of December 29, 1170. The great Norman transept where the murder took place was rebuilt about 1450. King Edward IV donated a beautiful royal window of stained glass showing the king kneeling at prayer with his family. The window dominated the whole transept. However, most of this priceless window glass was destroyed by the Puritan fanatics in 1642.

The cathedral contains the tombs of kings and queens, princes and princesses, pre-Reformation bishops of the Church of Rome, and not a few commoners who throughout the various ages were patrons of the Church. There is so much to see that it might be advisable to join up with an organized tour of Canterbury Cathedral. The knowledgeable guides will be of great help.

One is reminded of the early pilgrims who came on foot and as Chaucer put it, "from every shire's end of England to Canterbury they wend. . . ." There were no cars, buses, or trains. Their travel conditions were thoroughly primitive and their pilgrimage truly penitential. But they came to honor their saints and martyrs. Today we mostly travel in style, and penitential suffering is hard to achieve. Still, we can make a try at it.

MEDITATION

"What does it profit a man if he gain the whole world and lose his soul?" Both St. Thomas à Becket and St. Thomas More are reminders to us that we may be faced in our own lives with such a choice. Each saint challenged a king, turning his face against the comfortable life that agreement with the king offered. To go along with those in power guaranteed continued status, money, preference. Each made the moral choice from which, once made, there was no turning back from the hard road to martyrdom.

Not many of us will ever have to deal with such an enormous choice — and yet, in the lives of us all, there are times when tough choices must be made. Shall we go along with what the boss is doing, or shall we quit and put our family in financial jeopardy? Or maybe it's not even that drastic: Shall we go along, keep quiet about something we know is wrong, or speak out and risk an ugly confrontation? That might cause a small martyrdom, but meditating on Canterbury, we can pray that Our Lord will give us the courage to make the right choice and be able to accept our small martyrdoms.

CHAPTER THREE
Glastonbury

Glastonbury, on the Somerset plain, has a history of human habitation extending back through the unchartered mists of time. Glastonbury was once an island surrounded by marshes, with a mysterious conical hill called the Tor, and its history is entwined in layers of myth and legend. We do know that for the Celts, who lived there before the birth of Christ, it was a sacred place in which the dead could rest. To the Christian, it is the cradle of the faith in England, because modern archeologists show conclusively that ever since the fifth century it was the site of a Celtic monastery.

There are tales that connect King Arthur to Glastonbury and evidence that this ancient ruler did in fact exist. Among the most fascinating is the probability that he is buried there. Some old legends place Joseph of Arimathea at Glastonbury and still other stories relate that it is the burial place of St. Patrick.

It is quite certain that, from the eighth century on, there has been a tradition that connects St. Patrick with Glastonbury. Great numbers of Irish pilgrims made the difficult journey to visit what they believed to be his tomb. Modern excavations, however, have left it unclear whether the Glastonbury St. Patrick was the great apostle to Ireland or another of the same name.

The monastery such pilgrims visited was built

**Above: Artist's Concept of Original Glastonbury Abbey
Below: Modern Ruins of Glastonbury Abbey**

of wattle and twigs. It was a collection of huts and tiny chapels, with one larger chapel dedicated to Our Lady. Those who lived there were more hermits than monks.

The Saxons followed the Celts in the seventh century, and the Benedictine rule was introduced at Glastonbury. The Benedictine style of monastic life found a hospitable home and flourished there. Its Celtic origins were respected by the newcomers, and the ancient sacred places — the Church of Our Lady and the cemetery — were not set aside when improved buildings and a new church dedicated to St. Peter and St. Paul were erected. Those days of vigorous growth were followed by a decline caused mainly by the disturbances wrought by invading Danes. Peaceful times returned at last when St. Dunstan became abbot in 943. The revival he inspired spread from Glastonbury throughout the whole of England.

St. Dunstan was born near Glastonbury and had been a hermit there early in his life. The reforming movements, such as those at Cluny and other monastic centers, which had started on the European continent, became the model for Glastonbury. St. Dunstan nurtured the monastery and saw it flourish once again. He built a new church, a large cloister, and glass-and-metal furnaces. But even more importantly, he and the monks he trained revived virtually every medieval monastery in England. Because of them, Glastonbury Abbey was literally the motherhouse of English monastic life.

With William the Conqueror in 1066, the Saxon

abbots were deposed in favor of those who were Norman. Once again construction began; St. Dunstan's church was demolished but not the crude wattle-and-twig church of Our Lady. The cemetery and church retained their ancient sacred status until disaster struck in the form of a fire. Rebuilding began and, in 1186, a beautiful Lady Chapel stood on the exact site of the old wattle-and-twig church.

Inside the old church had stood a statue of Our Lady that survived the fire. Mary was pictured on the abbey coat of arms and on its seal. In one representation she is seated holding the child Jesus; in the other, Our Lady holds the child Jesus on one arm and in her other hand, a flowering bush, symbolic of Mary, Virgin and Mother. The bush has been described as the Glastonbury thorn, a sprig of which was thrust into the ground, according to legend, by Joseph of Arimathea. A more authenticated story relates the presenting of a rosary to adorn the statue by Queen Philippa, wife of King Edward III. The gift, made on the occasion of her pilgrimage to Glastonbury, had beads of gold and silver. Glastonbury also developed a special devotion to Joseph, an unusual interest in that time and place.

In the thirteenth, fourteenth, and fifteenth centuries, the monastery buildings were all completed — and Glastonbury Abbey was in its ascendancy, wielding powerful influence throughout the land. It had acquired vast estates and a remarkable library; it had also spearheaded innovative agricultural practices, including land-drainage techniques. Politically, the

41

abbot of Glastonbury was entitled to sit in the House of Lords. In 1524, Richard Whiting became abbot; his time was the turbulent years of Henry VII and Cromwell. Believing that the stormy years would pass, he arranged to hide away the abbey's treasures; but this led to his eventual imprisonment in the Tower of London, trial, and martyrdom. Blessed Richard Whiting and his companions were beatified by Pope Leo XIII in 1895.

The abbey was dissolved, the church stripped, and the buildings looted, even becoming a source of stone for the neighborhood. An observer with a discerning eye will spot many houses in and about Glastonbury adorned with carved pieces of abbey stone. The abbey became the property of a variety of owners, and eventually, through neglect and pillage, only the ruins stood. The Church of England rescued it by purchase in 1907 and reverently cares for the site. The area has been designated as having special national importance that should be preserved and enhanced; to that end, grants to aid repairs have been made.

Glastonbury today includes St. Mary's Chapel, the Abbey Church, St. Patrick's Chapel, and the Abbot's Kitchen. The ruined shell of St. Mary's Chapel stands in silent beauty. It dates from 1186, when it was rebuilt on the site of the burned wattle-and-twig church. This is the spot held holy as far back as can be determined — the original place of the wattle-and-twig church held as sacred by an endless stream of pilgrims.

The Abbey Church dates from the thirteenth century; the south wall and part of the north wall remain, which are sufficient to awe the visitor with an idea of the vast size the Abbey Church once had. The site of the altar and King Arthur's tomb are marked.

The Abbot's Kitchen was built in the fourteenth century; there, food for the abbot and his guests was prepared. It is in a fair state of preservation, and the inside as well as the outside can be viewed. It is a striking example of the medieval domed ceiling. St. Patrick's Chapel dates back to 1512, and one window contains some of the abbey's original stained glass.

The buildings lying outside the monastery enclosure (though owned by the abbey) did not suffer the same destructive fate, and many remain today, with some still in use.

St. Benedict's Church (also known as the Church of St. Benignus) dates from 1500, although changes and additions were made as recently as 1886. According to tradition, it is dedicated to an Irish saint who followed St. Patrick to Glastonbury.

The Tribunal is a courthouse that was also under the abbot's jurisdiction. It dates from the fifteenth century, although Abbot Bere replaced the front early in the sixteenth century. He was responsible for the windows that provided good light for the court proceedings. The Tribunal today has been carefully restored and houses a fascinating museum of abbey and town artifacts.

In the fifteenth century, when visitors were often too numerous to house at the monastery, a guesthouse was erected outside the abbey walls for their accommodation. This pilgrim inn still stands today as a haven for the visitor. Now called the George and Pilgrim Hotel, it is a highly ornamented example of medieval architecture.

St. John's Church was built in the fifteenth century and is made beautiful by its magnificent tower. It has a nave of seven bays, the arcades supported on pillars, and, above, a fine oak roof. Abbot Whiting's cope and gremial veil are preserved there. On either side of the sanctuary are the black marble tombs of local benefactors Richard and Joan Attwell, who died in the late fifteenth century. The side windows are fifteenth century. One depicts Mary; the other, Joseph of Arimathea.

St. Mary's Church and the Shrine of Our Lady of Glastonbury are of course modern. Consecrated in 1941, they stand just outside the enclosure of the abbey on land which formerly was the abbot's park. Although no one knows what became of the statue of Our Lady of Glastonbury after 1539, St. Mary's has a beautiful representation inspired by the design of the abbey seal. It also possesses a tapestry created by Brother Louis Barlow of Prinknash Abbey, a Benedictine foundation in Gloucestershire. This hangs over the high altar and pictures Blessed Richard Whiting and other saints associated with Glastonbury.

There are both Anglican and Roman Catholic pilgrimages to Glastonbury annually. It is a thriving market town, well able to care for visitors and pilgrims. Although it can no longer be reached directly by rail, it is fourteen miles from the main highway, M5. Traveling through the pleasant Somerset countryside, one can see Glastonbury from afar by catching sight of the Glastonbury Tor, a high hill topped by the ruined chapel of St. Michael the Archangel. The town is not far from places with delightful names like Cheddar Gorge or Wookey Hole, and it can be easily reached by bus from nearby cities steeped in ancient Roman history, including Bristol, Bath, and Wells.

Wells is called Somerset's cathedral city, a beautiful place spread beneath the rolling hills. The cathedral is a glory in stone, with its famous West Front and great clock. Dating from the thirteenth century is the celebrated St. Cuthbert's Church, almost as beautiful as the cathedral and boasting of a carved tie-beam roof. Also of interest to pilgrims or tourists are the old houses of The Vicar's Close — one of the oldest medieval streets in Europe. There is also the moated Bishop's Palace, where a new generation of swans has been taught to ring a bell when the birds want food.

Bath still retains its Roman heritage, although many of the health spas it thrived on are no more. It still has the "country" look about it, despite the fact that modern industry and technology have made inroads into its former serenity. It always had a reputation of being a quiet, restful place to visit. Again, there is much of real history in its streets and alleyways.

Bristol is a thriving port on the border with

Wales. Its efforts at urban renewal and its revival as the cultural center of the west of England make it an interesting and rewarding place to visit. It has some good older hotels and some modern ones, including an American-style Holiday Inn. Glastonbury is but an hour and a half away, and the roads are reasonably good. But don't expect a freeway all the way. Once out of Bristol, it's the normal English country road, narrow and slow — especially if one is caught behind a truck or farm vehicle. Still, it's worth the experience, and the countryside is beautiful.

Glastonbury Abbey is open to the public daily throughout the year: in December, from 9:30 A.M. to 4:30 P.M.; in January and November, from 9:30 A.M. to 5:00 P.M.; in February, from 9:30 A.M. to 5:30 P.M.; in March, April, and October, from 9:30 A.M. to 6:00 P.M.; in May and September, from 9:30 A.M. to 7:00 P.M.; and in June, July, and August, from 9:30 A.M. to 7:30 P.M. Admission for children under five is free. Those older pay 30 pence (approximately 75¢ U.S.), while adults are charged 60 pence ($1.50 U.S.).

There are special rates for parties of ten or over, and even season tickets are available for both individuals and families. In addition to the normal tourist guides, there are portable tape-recorded guides available at the gatehouse. They are highly recommended and add considerable enjoyment to the visit to the various chapels and halls.

Glastonbury is also a thriving English market town with over seven thousand inhabitants. Its main street is full of interesting shops specializing in arts, crafts, antiques, and local sheepskin goods for which it is famous worldwide. For those tourists or pilgrims who like walking and meditating, there are over eighty specially laid-out footpaths, many of which date back to the founding of Glastonbury Abbey and earlier. In a word, Glastonbury has been described as one of those pleasant little towns where past and present meet in harmony. Add to that its spiritual heritage — and one shouldn't miss it while in England.

MEDITATION

Our Lord told us, "Truly, I say to you, unless you turn and become like little children, you will never enter the kingdom of heaven" (Matthew 18:3). Can we learn to be childlike, as were the simple hermits who built a shrine to the Blessed Virgin in the only materials available to them: mud wattle and twigs? In our sophisticated lives, shaped by experts in art, color, and technique, do we have anything to compare with the sacred place preserved beyond its time even by those hostile to its creators? The all-embracing love the builders had for Our Lord, Our Lady, and — completing the Holy Family — St. Joseph, must have been visible in everything they touched. The atmosphere within the chapel walls must have breathed this love reaching out to any who entered — beautiful by virtue of the devotion in the hands of its builders, glorifying God and praising his Blessed Mother.

It's gone now, destroyed by an all-consuming

fire, and the church built on the very site stands to-day in ruins; but we can imagine the primitive chapel. We can see it still in our mind's eye and we can feel the atmosphere where men truly believed in the importance of love: "This is my commandment, that you love one another as I have loved you" (John 15:12). We can learn from its builders that what matters is not how imposing and awe-inspiring our works are but rather how well we used the talents and materials God provided for us.

The pilgrimage to Glastonbury will show us churches, public buildings, and ruins whose craftsmanship will seem incredible; but perhaps we will learn most from contemplating that which we will not see: the long-gone wattle-and-twig Lady Chapel. Thinking about it might help each of us see greater meaning in our own quiet lives.

CHAPTER FOUR

Santiago de Compostela

In the harsh northwestern coastal part of Spain called Galicia lies the shrine that stood proudly with Rome and Jerusalem as the medieval pilgrims' goal. In this rugged land, which is surprisingly Celtic, people wear a variety of kilt, love their bagpipes, and honor their traditions. It never was an easy place to get to; thus the pilgrim who successfully made the journey would wear a cockleshell so that all the world would know he had been to Santiago de Compostela.

The name Santiago de Compostela has interesting origins. Compostela is composed of two words meaning "countryside of the shining star." The name James in Latin is Jacobus; in Old Spanish, Iago; hence, Sant-Iago. St. James is the patron saint of Spain and Santiago de Compostela his historic shrine.

After the death of Christ, the Apostles fulfilled the great commission of the risen Savior: "Go therefore and make disciples of all nations, baptizing them in the name of the Father and of the Son and of the Holy Spirit" (Matthew 28:19). According to Spanish tradition, St. James the Greater came to Spain and preached the Gospel. As a proof that the tradition is based on fact, it is said that his relics were found in the ninth century.

The stories were an important part of Spanish culture and belief. It was particular devotion to the

Cathedral of Santiago de Compostela

Apostle who had brought Christianity to their land that gave Spaniards the motivation to free themselves from domination by the Moors. Modern scholars cast doubt on the authenticity of the claims about St. James, but there can be no doubt that the tradition filled the people with pride in their Christian faith and courage to protect it.

In the ninth century, King Alfonso II (who was resisting the Muslims who had overrun Spain) built a stone church to replace the wooden one over the tomb of St. James. This made it easier for people to come and honor the saint. About fifty years later, the popularity of the pilgrimage led to the building of an even larger and more impressive church. At the end of the tenth century, Compostela was destroyed by al-Mansur al Allah. In 1075, King Alfonso VI built the present central part of the cathedral. In the twelfth century, most of the remainder was completed, although there have been additions and changes down through the centuries. During the Middle Ages, whatever the politics and turmoil, Santiago de Compostela flourished as a sacred place.

The city of Santiago de Compostela looks today remarkably as it did hundreds of years ago. Twenty years ago, in a special Holy Year, two and a half million pilgrims made their way there from all corners of the globe. Pilgrim routes to Santiago de Compostela from France were established as early as the tenth century. Eventually hostels and hospices were erected along the routes to assist pilgrims in need.

The routes became known as "The Way of St.

James," and various languages were heard as the people walked along. The majority of the pilgrims were always from outside Spain. In fact, most were French, with a smattering from every other nation in Europe. The usual pilgrimage would form up in groups at Tour St. Jacques, on the right bank of the Seine River, near Notre Dame in Paris. The journey was almost nine hundred miles, so people banded themselves together: royalty, beggars, businessmen, knights, clergy, brigands, and the strolling players. In every pilgrimage there were always the devout or those who wanted to make their peace with God. The knights in attendance had probably promised to make the pilgrimage if they succeeded in battle. There were even criminals, openly going on pilgrimage as the sentence from a judge. There are many reports of a judge telling a guilty man that he would be spared prison if he went to Compostela. Proof of the journey was demanded, and the sentenced criminal would have to bring back a certificate from the shrine stating that he had indeed arrived. Human nature being what it is, this led to abuses, with some people making quite a business out of bogus certificates issued en route.

The number of pilgrims to the shrine of St. James kept growing as the centuries passed, with two hundred thousand a year being recorded up through the sixteenth century.

Santiago de Compostela is unique in that it is the only other place besides Rome which is allowed a Church Holy Year. Whenever July 25 falls on a Sunday, that year is a Holy Year for the Spanish shrine, and thousands of Europeans and Hispanics from other hemispheres make the Holy Year pilgrimage. For the native Spanish too, the Holy Year is something special, and several million will visit the shrine, petitioning St. James, the patron of Spain.

Great ceremonies are held in the cathedral, and a papal legate is appointed by the Holy Father to preside. In conjunction with the Holy Year, symposiums are organized on Church teachings, music, and the arts. Leading scholars from all over the world attend the sessions, which are held in the famous University of Santiago, one of the oldest educational institutes in Europe.

The focal point of any pilgrimage there is the cathedral, which was built on the site of the tomb of St. James. It also houses Spain's most sacred relic, the arm of St. James, which lies in a special chapel. To see the Cathedral of St. James very much as the medieval pilgrim did, approach it via the Plaza de las Platerias and you will see a stately Romanesque building with a huge bell tower. If you go around to the eastern plaza, you will see the magnificent Puerta Sancta — the Holy Door — opened only during the years of special pilgrimages. The door has carved figures of the Apostles and prophets, and, in the middle, Santiago himself dressed as a pilgrim with the big hat, gourd, and cockleshell. The door dates from 1694, when the Portuguese sculptor Pedro del Compo was commissioned to do it.

Inside the cathedral is a wealth of medieval art,

the work of master artists. There are figures of Christ enthroned, St. James as a workman, and various angels; there is also a depiction of the Tree of Jesse from which Jesus sprang. Other biblical motifs include, for example, figures of Hosea and Obadiah. Apostles are present: Peter holding the keys, Bartholomew preaching; only Judas is missing.

One of the most extraordinary and remarkable objects associated with the Cathedral of St. James is the *botafumeiro*, a silver-plated iron censer about three feet high. When it is used, as on the feast of St. James, a two-hundred-foot-long heavy hemp rope extends from the highest part of the building through a complicated system of pulleys and eventually drops down to the censer. There, it is passed through a very large ring and securely fastened. Eight men grasp and pull the object up into the air. Charcoal and incense are placed inside, and the priest gives the *botafumeiro* its initial push. The men pull hard; the *botafumeiro* swings up ninety feet to the ceiling and with a frightening *swish!* swings back down over the heads of the congregation.

Several years ago, I was visiting the Cathedral of St. James with a group of U.S. bishops. The local archbishop was showing us around the cathedral and had arranged a special swinging of the *botafumeiro*, just for his American visitors. We all stood in front of the high altar, right on the edge of the sanctuary. As the *botafumeiro* swung from side to side, soaring high into the ceiling, it kept coming closer and closer to the line of prelates and myself. Suddenly one of the bishops, well known by his confreres for handling financial affairs, turned to the host archbishop and exclaimed, "I hope you have insurance." The remark brought the church down.

The shrine of Compostela is not just known for its architectural beauty. There is a continuing spiritual tale to tell of healings, miracles, and individual renewal, brought about through pilgrimage, prayer, and penance. Among the visitors to the shrine were Charlemagne, King Alfonso II, El Cid Campeador, Louis VII of France, St. Francis of Assisi, James III of Scotland and England, and in more contemporary times, Angelo Roncalli, patriarch of Venice, who soon after became Pope John XXIII.

Santiago de Compostela is situated in one of the most beautiful parts of Spain, the northwest. It is near the Atlantic coast and not far from La Coruña, one of Europe's most westerly points. There is good air service from Madrid and Barcelona; trains and buses enter the city from all over the country. The roads are very good, so traveling by car does not become a boring chore. Indeed, from Madrid you can stop at Ávila (St. Theresa's shrine), or Segovia, Salamanca, and Zamora, and still make it in a day. En route there are plenty of accommodations, in both hotels and *pensiónes* (boardinghouses). In the major Spanish cities, the hotels are smaller but certainly on par with the better American ones — and the service is often much better. Sometimes the only problem is language, although in the major cities most employees speak good English.

One thing you have to note in Spain, as in other parts of Europe, is the fact that mealtimes are scheduled at later hours than in the U.S. If you're leaving very early, remember that breakfast won't be served before 8:00 A.M., lunch not before 1:00 P.M., and dinner around 8:00 P.M. at the earliest. You can get dinner service at a good restaurant up to eleven at night and sometimes later.

In Santiago de Compostela, there are a number of good hotels, plenty of *pensiónes*, and a few religious guesthouses. Of particular delight is the lovely, nationally owned Hostal de los Reyes Católicos. Having the famous university within its midst, it is a cap-and-gown town. There are shops, restaurants, and bars catering mainly to students, and there are similar places catering to pilgrims and tourists. But nothing stops a person from crossing into the university sector.

The city is worth exploring, and it can't be done in a day. There is so much to see, whether cultural, artistic, or religious. And much of it speaks of the history of the past eleven hundred years. Make sure your camera is working because you are in for a treat. There are so many fine buildings and monuments to record on film that you can spend many years to come explaining to relatives and friends the religious history of this quiet countryside which reminds many of Scotland or the State of Washington in the U.S.

Again, make arrangements through a reliable travel agent. Get a book on the area out of your local library. One of the best for this part of Europe is James Michener's *Iberia: Spanish Travels and Reflections*. He traveled St. James's Way several times, and the descriptive beauty of his writings on Galicia is worth the time it takes to digest the book. This is a highly recommended shrine to visit, for both spiritual and aesthetic reasons.

MEDITATION

Reading and learning about ancient traditions and legends may sometimes leave a modern skeptic wondering how on earth intelligent people believed all this. We must try to put ourselves back in a time before the advent of the scientific mind when having a frightful cold meant being healed only because nature — that is, nature and nature's God — managed it. Getting well could seem like a miracle. When travel meant facing rat-infested boats and bandit-plagued highways, getting somewhere safely was a miracle. Can we deny it? To go from these life experiences to tales of an Apostle finding his way from Jerusalem to Spain seemed like just another miracle in an age of miracles.

St. James the Greater's reason for coming — to convert the pagan — was an ideal reason for daring to undertake such a journey. The Spanish caught up in this ideal became great evangelizers. Part of the reason they supported Christopher Columbus was to spread the Gospel. In the little village on the island of Majorca where Junípero Serra was born, he and many other young men had the vision of bringing

Christ to the Indians. As he walked through California with the Spanish army, Serra preached the Good News.

It is a great tradition: that as Christ has been received by us, we must spread his teaching to all the world. When did you last talk about Jesus to someone who has no church? When did you last explain what the faith is all about to someone who asked a question? Aren't we all a little afraid of it? Yet, it was the commission of the risen Christ that we share the Good News, not keep it all to ourselves.

Perhaps, as modern scholars insist, there is more legend than fact in the story of Santiago; but the Spanish knew its true purpose. From our contemplation of the meaning of this shrine of great antiquity, we might well pray to be less self-conscious and more sharing of our beliefs.

CHAPTER FIVE

Our Lady of the Pillar

Spain's Zaragoza (or Saragossa) is a city rich in history. Its culture has evolved from its domination by the Iberians at the dawn of civilization, then by the Romans who established a colony there, followed by the Arabs who conquered Zaragoza and stayed there for centuries, and finally its formation by Christianity.

Spain has actually been Christian since Roman times. St. Paul planned to take the Gospel there, and it is even possible that he may have succeeded. According to tradition, James the Apostle is a patron of Spain because, despite the perils of travel, he is said to have made a missionary journey to the Iberian peninsula. There, in the time of the Romans, he spread the Gospel and converted the populace. According to legend, in the midst of this difficult work, Our Lady appeared to him on the shores of the Ebro River and gave him encouragement. She reached out and handed him the very stone on which she stood as a symbol of the enduring faith of the people of Aragón. The symbolism is reminiscent of Simon being renamed Peter. The Basilica of Our Lady of the Pillar (in Spanish, Nuestra Señora del Pilar), which was built next to the river, commemorates the event. It is on the site of the earlier Visigothic church that was destroyed by fire in 1434. The statue of Our Lady of El Pilar, as it is also known, was saved and is enshrined in the ba-

Basilica of Our Lady of the Pillar

silica. It is a devotional reminder of steadfastness in the face of persecution and difficulty.

The Christian community planted at that early time did indeed prove to have enduring faith. During the Roman period, its members suffered unbelievable persecutions and martyrdom but persevered in the faith. In the fourth century, St. Engracia and others went to their death rather than deny Our Lord. When the Arabs conquered the city, it was yielded only on condition that the Christians and their churches would not be interfered with. The people were prepared to hold out without this concession.

When the Christians regained Zaragoza, its cathedral was erected on the site of the former Muslim mosque. King Ferdinand and Queen Isabella established their court in the beautiful Arab palace, la Aljaferia.

The visitor to the Basilica of Our Lady of El Pilar might be surprised to find that it is a daily place of pilgrimage for thousands. The basilica is constantly crowded with individuals and family groups who wait patiently for an opportunity to get close to the shrine. It is especially important that the children receive the blessings of this pilgrimage. For many Spanish families, the rite of First Holy Communion is not complete without a visit to the Virgin of El Pilar. The children are brought to the shrine, many in the traditional dress of their native region. After Mass, the children are photographed individually with the statue of the Madonna as background.

The chapel shrine of Nuestra Señora del Pilar is

only one part of this enormous basilica. One could spend all day and not cover every historical side chapel and monument that is within it. Starting on the outside, there is the tremendous square frequented by thousands of pigeons whose survival is guaranteed. Vendors sell the food to the pilgrims who delight in feeding the birds. From this square one can see the ten domes of the basilica all adorned with colored tiles. The central dome is enormous, and the four towers of the rectangular building reach impressively toward the sky. Once inside, one notices the long wide naves and the huge square pillars that separate them. The Pilar shrine stands alone in the center. It has three sculptured altars, one of which houses the famous statue of Our Lady of the Pillar. Interesting enough is the fact that the statue is not very large — a golden-toned wood carving about twenty inches in height, standing on an embroidered base with a jeweled monstrancelike backdrop at the head.

The main altar of the basilica is ancient, having been saved from the old Visigothic church that preceded it. It was said to have been sculptured in alabaster by Damian Forment in the early sixteenth century. It is considered to be one of the great artistic treasures now in Spain. From the inside we discover that the great central dome was painted by Goya, as was the vault of the beautiful choir of the basilica. Flemish and Spanish tapestries abound within the walls, and the sacristy is rich in art and carved wood. Its size outdoes some churches you might have seen in your travels, and its floor has a unique marble design.

Close by the Pilar basilica is the see of Zaragoza, the cathedral seat of the archbishop. It was built on land formerly occupied by a very rich Arab mosque. When the city was retaken by Christian armies, the cathedral was named after Our Savior. It was formerly of Romanesque design but was rebuilt in the early fourteenth century. The new edifice was of Gothic design and took a century to complete. Of the remains of the original church, only the apse on the Gospel side is still preserved. The various chapels contain tombs of saints and patrons of the cathedral, and much of the artwork is vastly superior to that contained in El Pilar. Some of the paintings and sculpture are from Italian, Flemish, and Spanish schools of the fourteenth, fifteenth, and sixteenth centuries. The grand sacristy contains a medieval cupboard with marble and alabaster busts as well as fine gold monstrances and chalices.

Tragically, the Cathedral of Our Lady of El Pilar is in constant need of repair, and one can sense the dilemma of church authorities: Because the basilica is the main attraction, needed funds must be spread out thin. The cathedral exterior is almost as magnificent as the interior. The artisans involved in its construction knew how to make a thing of beauty for the glory of God.

These two splendid churches would be enough to gain the attention of pilgrims or tourists for several days. However, there is much more in Zaragoza, since it is the product of several civilizations: Iberian, Roman, Muslim, and Christian. According to legend, it was founded by the grandson of Noah, a man called Tubal. It was then a settlement called Salduba. When the Romans arrived, they named it Caesarea Augusta after their emperor, Augustus. It grew into a city that eventually was renamed by the Arab conquerors as Sarakosta (actually a corruption of Caesarea Augusta). When the Christians reconquered the area, its present name was adopted. The city not only became an important center for Spanish commerce and learning, it also became the court of the Aragón kings, and thé celebrated royal couple Ferdinand and Isabella resided there. It suffered during the Peninsular Wars and it was partially destroyed by the French under Napoleon. Today, Zaragoza is one of the main cities of Spain, with a strong economic and industrial base.

But for the pilgrim or tourist this ancient city still retains its historic heritage, and monuments to Zaragoza's past can be found all over the place. The filigreed walls of so many buildings are the gift of past artisans whose great skills and love of beauty are so evident. There is the Dean's Archway, hidden in an alleyway, bridging two sections of a sixteenth-century building. Then there is the fourteenth-century church of St. Mary Magdalen, with its baroque portal and magnificent high altar. There are many more such religious and secular monuments that can absorb one's attention for days — if one could spare them. Needless to say, the fascinating city of Zaragoza makes a worthwhile visit for either the pilgrim or the tourist.

What's the best way of getting there? There are several airlines, both foreign and domestic, that offer direct flights from the U.S. to Madrid and Barcelona. Once in Spain, there are a number of options available. You may take buses from Madrid or Barcelona, or the domestic Spanish airline flights that depart several times daily. There are also good car rental rates; however, as we have mentioned before — arrange for European rentals back in the U.S. before you leave so that you not only save money but are assured of a car.

Zaragoza has a lot of good hotels, some expensive and some quite reasonable. There are also moderate *pensiónes* for those with simple tastes. Restaurants are all over the place, with international menus or simple local fare. Whatever you choose, it's all good; but don't expect to be eating Mexican style, as Spanish and Mexican food have very little in common. There are also places with a touch of home for the U.S. visitors. After all, some of our servicemen are stationed at air installations in the region, and Zaragoza is a favorite rest-and-recreation place for them.

Of course, if you want to go with a group — and this is the cheaper way to go — consult a travel agent. The agents know the best places to stay and where the best restaurants are. They will also arrange tours of the religious shrines and other places of interest. Conducted tours on pilgrimages to Europe normally have a priest with them, and so the spiritual side of the trip is well taken care of. If you are responding to a group tour or pilgrimage advertisement, make sure to check on the advertiser — whether it be an individual or a travel agent — before you part with your deposit money. In most cases, there's nothing to worry about; but there is always the possibility of being the victim of a travel scam, so it is wise to play it safe. Wherever you see the ad, whether it's in a magazine or newspaper or on TV, it's sensible to check with the local Better Business Bureau. If it is a mailed solicitation, do the same in the city of origin.

One thing for certain: A visit to Zaragoza can be an enjoyable spiritual and cultural exercise — a once-in-a-lifetime experience or something to be repeated.

MEDITATION

". . . Every one who acknowledges me before men, I also will acknowledge before my Father who is in heaven" (Matthew 10:32). Jesus spoke those words to all of us, and the whole history of the Church shows people who held them close to the heart and suffered persecution rather than deny Our Lord. Peter weakened on one occasion but, according to one story, later persevered to the point of giving up his life on the cross. The people of Aragón held on to the faith, and the legendary story simply confirms it. Making this pilgrimage causes us to meditate on the words of Jesus and the sad truth that persecution is with us still. Today there are Christians suffering in eastern Europe, in Africa, the Middle East, and some parts of Asia. They may not be thrown to the lions nor torn limb from limb, but effective means are used against them to ensure as much misery as possible in their lives.

These are people who need our prayers, who should have a place in our thoughts daily. It's so easy in our safe, protected land to turn aside unpleasant stories of persecuted people. These, despite distance and language barriers, are truly our neighbors — and if we don't speak for the voiceless, who will? Perhaps letter-writing campaigns or organized protests are not my cup of tea; does that then mean that I am excused from all participation? A different world cannot be made by indifferent people. I can pray with unceasing fervor that those who are urged to deny Christ publicly will have the God-given strength to declare him publicly instead. Then perhaps, by my daily words and actions in my own tight little world, I'll find I'm doing the same thing. What a terrific promise Jesus has made, that he will declare to the Father that I belong to him!

CHAPTER SIX

Lourdes

Lourdes is truly the most famous of the world-wide Marian shrines. There, the Blessed Virgin appeared to a humble French shepherd girl eighteen times, from February to April in 1858. The apparitions had a profound effect not only on the visionary, Bernadette Soubirous, but also on the universal Church. Miracles at the Lourdes shrine have been authenticated by the Church, which also canonized the girl whom we now know as St. Bernadette. As always, Mary's message in such apparitions — wherever they have been authenticated — is the same: She tells those with whom she graces her presence to pray and do penance for world peace.

Lourdes is a small town at the foot of the Pyrénées in southwest France. When Bernardette was born there on January 7, 1844, it had a population of four thousand that struggled to make a living on its marble and slate quarries and the surrounding agricultural areas.

It was a life of privation for the Soubirous family, and to make matters worse, Bernadette came down with cholera at about age eleven. It was a time of epidemic — in a few months, more than thirty victims died in Lourdes. Even though she recovered, Bernadette bore the scars of the disease for the whole of her young life. As somebody said later on, the disease weakened her body but at the same time "tem-

American Express Travel Service Photo

Lourdes Grotto

pered her soul." And, as Bernadette later observed, she perceived the hardships as trials that God was subjecting her to, noting that "when you know the Lord wants it that way you don't complain."

But poor health was not the only difficulty in Bernadette's life: She and her family suffered the hardships that were endured through lack of employment. Often they did not have the bare necessities of life — even shelter. At one point they existed by living in a dismal, abandoned prison that measured approximately twelve feet by twelve feet. In this dread, dank environment, the young girl — who could neither read nor write — succeeded in developing her cheerful, pleasant personality.

Not long after moving into the prison hole, Bernadette, her sister, and a cousin took a long walk in the rain in search of firewood. They spotted a little pile on the other side of the Gave River. Two of the youngsters rushed into the icy water after removing their shoes and socks, but Bernadette was hesitant about following them into the chilly river. At a noise that seemed like the wind, she raised her eyes and looked in the direction of a grotto, or cave. Inside the grotto she saw a woman dressed in white with a rose at either foot. In her hands she clasped a white rosary, and Bernadette immediately put her hand into her pocket and withdrew her own. The woman, who would turn out to be Our Lady, then raised her rosary and crossed herself, and Bernadette did the same. This was the first of eighteen visions as Bernadette herself recounted it. Later in the day when her family learned of her experience, it was dismissed as the effect of illness and fever, and Bernadette was forbidden to visit the grotto. Three days later her father reluctantly permitted her to return to the grotto, and there, while reciting the Rosary, the Lady appeared once more.

The family was now very upset with Bernadette, especially since gossip about her spread through the village. Onlookers began to gather when word came that Bernadette was going to pray in the grotto, but she herself never revealed details of many of her meetings. Finally, the civil authorities became concerned about these large gatherings and brought Bernadette in for questioning. It was an unpleasant experience for Bernadette, who insisted they were twisting her words and refused to sign any statement. They did, however, extract a promise from her frightened father that she would not be allowed to return to the grotto. Her confessor assured her that the civil officials had gone too far. The seventh apparition then occurred on Tuesday, February 23. Two days later, during the ninth apparition, a miraculous spring came forth after Bernadette dug out the soil with her own two hands. The Lady had directed her to go and cleanse herself at the spring; unable to find any water, Bernadette scratched at the soil and found first mud and then a gushing spring.

The crowds were growing, and so were the threats from the civil authorities. Walking out from Mass, Bernadette was met by police who took her off for more questions, bullying, and threats.

The crowds and the visions continued, and at the conclusion of the thirteenth apparition, on March 2, a much-shaken Bernadette confided that the Lady had given her a fearful task. She was to tell the clergy to come to the grotto in procession and to erect a chapel there. The clergy responded by demanding to know the name of the Lady. When Bernadette admitted she did not know it, she was told she had to ask. During the fourteenth vision, on behalf of the priests, she asked, but her only answer was a smile. After being asked again and again, during the sixteenth vision, the Lady revealed to Bernadette in words totally foreign to the semiliterate girl, "I am the Immaculate Conception."

In late March, three doctors were sent for in an attempt to certify that Bernadette was unbalanced and should be committed to a mental institution. That they did not do, although they stated that she was suffering from an unspecified "illness."

Bernadette continued to live her simple, unassuming life and, on June 3, received her First Holy Communion. About two weeks later, on July 16, Bernadette saw the Holy Virgin, as she now called her during this eighteenth and last vision. In October 1858, the grotto, which had been closed by local authorities, was opened by order of Napoleon III. With the hope of regaining her health, Bernadette was admitted as an indigent to a hospice run by the Sisters of Nevers.

The Church continued investigating all that had happened at Lourdes. In 1861, the bishop purchased the grotto and the surrounding land. Then, on January 18, 1862, the bishop of Tarbes declared that ". . . the Immaculate Mary, the Mother of God, really appeared to Bernadette." Thus the faithful were assured that the Church also accepted the wondrous events as true.

In 1866, after living with them for years in their hospice, Bernadette began her novitiate with the Sisters of Nevers at the Convent of Saint-Gildard. She pronounced her final vows in September of 1878 and died, still a young woman, the following April.

Today, on the very place where the Virgin asked for a chapel, stand three magnificent basilicas, one dedicated to the Immaculate Conception, one to the Rosary, and one to Pope St. Pius X. The ground for these impressive buildings was broken soon after the bishop of Tarbes had acknowledged that the visions were authentic. Where the Virgin had called for "prayer and penance," pilgrims now flock to follow her wish. The Virgin had told Bernadette that many pilgrims would come to Lourdes, but the simple, unaffected young girl would never have imagined today's millions of visitors nor the sights that greet them from the moment they first enter the town.

On arrival, the average visitor is surprised to find really two entities — the city itself and the shrine area. The city is like any other small town in the countryside, trying to stave off what some would call progress. The small-town charm of Lourdes is still there, even though its main street has a cluttered look made by a mixture of the ancient and the modern.

Most of the hotels are within walking distance of the grotto and other shrines, although tour groups tend to be bused around. The reason for this is that group leaders have normally reserved places at various ceremonies and they start punctually. No one in Lourdes appreciates latecomers, whether it be for meals or Mass, the bus rendezvous or the Rosary.

Pilgrims previously have heard about the grotto at Lourdes, and it's probably the first place they head for upon arrival. There can be found evidence of the many miracles attributed to the Blessed Virgin's intercession — among them, crutches hanging from the ceiling of the grotto where Bernadette first experienced the apparitions. Hundreds at a time pray before the statue of the Virgin while lighted candles adorn its base. But the main thing people notice about the grotto is its atmosphere of peace. There is a certain, unspoken "hush" about the place, and this is continued even at the most vocal of the prayer services held several times a day. This "hush" actually permeates the rest of the huge shrine area and is something that can only be explained by the fact that Lourdes is a site of continuous prayer and penitential acts.

From the city, one crosses over the Gave River to the magnificent esplanade, where on one side is the Hospital of Notre Dame and on the other the ruins of an ancient castle.

Up ahead, close to where Our Lady had asked for a chapel stand the three great basilicas mentioned earlier. The Immaculate Conception Basilica was built on the rock above the grotto and took eight years to build, being completed in 1870. The Rosary Basilica was started as part of the twenty-fifth anniversary of the apparitions in 1883. There was also a practical motive — an ever-growing number of pilgrims were flocking to the shrine and one church was not sufficient to accommodate them all. This basilica has a basic Byzantine interior, with the four arms of the Greek cross and fifteen chapels dedicated to the various mysteries of the Rosary.

The Basilica of St. Pius X is a huge underground church located on the left of the esplanade. It can hold twenty-five thousand people and is used often as a substitute for the area in front of the Rosary Basilica, especially during bad weather. It took twelve years to build, using the most modern structural techniques. It was dedicated in March 1958 by the then Cardinal Angelo Roncalli, who in the same year became Pope John XXIII.

Although Lourdes is in an isolated part of France, it is by no means isolated from the rest of the world. There is an international airport at nearby Tarbes — nothing luxurious; in fact, it is rather austere, but with a runway capable of receiving the largest of jumbo jets. And the jumbo jets do arrive in great numbers from all over the world. Most of them are chartered by national pilgrim groups. There are several domestic French airline flights in and out of Tarbes each day, with an increased schedule in the summer months. There is also very good train service from Paris, Bordeaux, and Toulouse. In addition, there are several so-called "White Trains" to convey the sick and the handicapped pilgrims who are part of national pilgrimages to the shrine. These have the most up-to-date equipment and medical facilities available and are normally staffed by medical volunteers, including doctors, nurses, and technicians.

Going by road is also easy from any part of France or western Europe. The major roads are fast, with easy on-and-off access. Of course, one cannot expect an expressway all the way to Lourdes, but between the most important cities on the way there are good four-lane highways. Rent-a-car facilities are available, including all the better-known American companies. It is advisable to make reservations in the U.S. before leaving on the trip. Not only is it cheaper (an important consideration), but it ensures that you do have a car when you need it.

What about accommodations? In Lourdes there are plenty, although few can be called first-class in the American sense. They cater to pilgrims; therefore, they are mostly rooms of double occupancy and few frills. The bonus is that in the majority of places you will enjoy delightful French country cuisine. The rates are very reasonable, even for pilgrims traveling on their own.

What's the best way to travel to Lourdes? The first rule is to go through a travel agent: Let the agent know whether you want to go alone, as a family, or with a group. Unless you intend to go only to Lourdes, you'll find that it is included on the itinerary of many attractive pilgrimages, which can include

Rome, the Holy Land, or the Marian shrines of Europe. Naturally, group touring is cheaper; but at the same time, it is more regimented than going alone or as a family. However, let the travel agent know your plans and he or she will try to get the best price possible. One note of caution: Be careful of private-group pilgrimages to anywhere, unless a recognized agent or major airline is involved.

The ceremonies at the shrine go on all day. Masses are available in most of the major languages from dawn to dusk. Pilgrims on their own should consult the various bulletin boards which publish such information daily. Group pilgrims will also find the same information at their hotel along with the daily schedule of the pilgrimage. Specially colorful are the Masses for various national groups, with congregations all dressed up in their particular countries' traditional dress.

Another moving daily ceremony is the late-afternoon healing service for the sick and handicapped. It starts from the grotto, with a priest or bishop carrying the Blessed Sacrament in a monstrance followed by a procession of the sick in wheelchairs aided by mostly volunteer attendants. Behind them are other pilgrims walking and singing hymns. When the procession reaches the esplanade, the celebrant passes with the monstrance through an avenue of stretchers and wheelchairs while he blesses the sick and other pilgrims in attendance. This momentous event is one of the most crowded ceremonies in the shrine area.

But probably the most moving of the Lourdes

ceremonies is the *"aux flambeaux"* (that is, with candles) rosary procession, which takes place every evening. It starts at the grotto, where all the national groups form up. Candles are lighted, and thousands of pilgrims march up and down the esplanade reciting the Rosary led by a leader-priest, with different languages being used for each decade. The Credo is recited and Marian hymns sung during the procession, which lasts about an hour. The shrine area is usually dark except where the candles carried by the pilgrims give some illumination. But on many occasions, when participants of major pilgrimages are in attendance, there is the "festival of light" at the end of the rosary procession. Suddenly, all of the outside lights of the basilicas and other shrines are turned on and further enhance the splendor and majesty of the moment.

Not to be forgotten when visiting Lourdes are the baths, or pools, where the sick and handicapped are immersed daily. Doctors and nurses — all volunteers, as are most of the lay attendants — are present to assist. People who are well are also encouraged to use the baths, and most do. For those pilgrims who are seriously ill, there is a fine hospital to tend to their every need right in the shrine area. There is always hope for a miracle cure and there have been some. But the Church is very careful about authenticating such claims, which must be certified by the medical bureau of Lourdes besides other doctors and clergy.

At Lourdes too is an impressive Way of the Cross with life-size bronze figures depicting each of the Stations. It is well used by pilgrims, as the Way of the Cross is considered one of the many penitential acts available in Lourdes. It can be said with certainty that the original message of the Virgin of Lourdes — calling for prayer and penance, as told to Bernadette — has well and truly been heeded by millions of the faithful in the more than a century and a quarter since Our Lady first appeared to Bernadette Soubirous.

MEDITATION

Jesus came to tell the Good News to the poor, to free the prisoner, to comfort the sorrowing — and in the story of Bernadette we have another sign of his ongoing concern for the most despairing lives. Jesus gave the gift of knowing his Blessed Mother to a girl so poor that she had neither proper food nor warmth; to a girl who lived as a prisoner might in a dark and dank cell; to a girl whose life lacked all the comforts and pleasures that the rest of us take for granted. To this ailing young child who hadn't yet received her First Holy Communion, God showed love and blessed her days. Bernadette understood God's love and his care — her very words of acceptance of ill health show us that. From this simple saint, we, in our much more protected lives, can learn that whatever problems come, whatever losses occur, God cares.

The pilgrims who flock to Lourdes also know better than most people on earth that the spiritual graces of the trip begin before they, the pilgrims, ever leave home and continue long after. What is important is acknowledging that one's life is important to God and that he is holding us upright through dark days and nights.

Lourdes and the story of Bernadette bring home to us the truth of the words of Jesus that not even a sparrow falls to the ground without God's awareness and that he knows us so well that every hair on our head is numbered (see Matthew 10:29-30). What a strong reminder that if God's eye is on the sparrow, then it surely is on us! God cares for us, however obscure we may feel ourselves to be and however powerless we may seem to the world. We have a powerful friend who has assured us, "Whoever does the will of God is my brother, and sister, and mother" (Mark 3:35).

CHAPTER SEVEN

Miraculous Medal Shrine

The story of the Miraculous Medal shrine is part of an unending history of divine intervention into the affairs of this world, in which Christ and his Blessed Mother work through ordinary human beings to help reshape mankind to the image and likeness of God.

The ordinary human being associated with this shrine was a postulant at the Daughters of Charity motherhouse at the Rue du Bac on the Left Bank in Paris, France. Catherine Labouré, the young postulant, was born on May 2, 1806, in the small village of Fain-les-Moutiers, in Burgundy province, one of seventeen children of Pierre and Madeleine Louise Labouré. They were a reasonably comfortable farm family, although, as was fairly typical, Catherine had no formal education.

However, from early childhood Catherine was known to attend daily Mass and receive Communion. She was remembered for having a prayer life that was above the ordinary. Tragedy entered her quiet life when she was nine and her mother died. It was then that her devotion to the Blessed Virgin is said to have increased. At age fourteen she and her twelve-year-old sister, Antoinette, took over the family housekeeping chores. It was well understood in the family that from a very early age Catherine had wanted to enter the religious life. Her father was opposed to this and, in 1828, sent her to Paris to work for his brother

Miraculous Medal Shrine

as a waitress in a café. The unhappy Catherine didn't stay long at that job; rather, she fulfilled her greatest desire by joining the Daughters of Charity in 1830.

While she was at the novitiate, spiritual wonders began. She experienced visions of St. Vincent de Paul, the founder of her order, and she revealed this to her confessor. She also told him that she enjoyed the visible presence of Christ in the Blessed Sacrament. He was her confessor and could not reveal any of this; by this time, after six months at the novitiate, Catherine was considered to be just an ordinary but shy religious. She seemed like a simple peasant girl with little education and typical country ways. Everything suddenly changed for her on the night of July 18, 1830.

She was awakened from a deep sleep by a young boy dressed in white who stood at her bedside telling her, "The Blessed Virgin awaits you!" She was led to the chapel where Our Lady appeared. While Catherine knelt before her, the Virgin gave her spiritual advice, predicted that calamities would befall the world, and told Catherine that she (Catherine) would be given a special mission. In later years, writing about this vision, Catherine said the Virgin "disappeared like a shadow, as she had come." The child, who she believed was her guardian angel, escorted her back to her room. She again revealed the vision to her confessor who, from all appearances, must have been a skeptical man, since he failed to take Catherine's story seriously.

Four months later, Catherine had a second apparition, on November 27, in which the Virgin revealed that a special mission would be entrusted to the future nun. The community was in the convent chapel for evening silent prayer when Catherine heard the same rustling sound of a dress that had marked the previous appearance of the Virgin. She looked at the altar and saw Mary standing on a snake which was coiled around a globe. Light streamed from the Virgin's hands, and surrounding her were the words "O Mary, conceived without sin, pray for us who have recourse to thee."

Catherine was instructed to have a medal struck depicting the apparition, and she told her confessor what the Virgin had said. The confessor still was not impressed, and the matter of the medal was not acted upon. Our Lady appeared to Catherine three more times in the next year, finally expressing her disappointment at the lack of action on the medal. Catherine again told the confessor of the Virgin's displeasure. This made the priest uneasy and, without breaking the seal of confession, he related the story of the apparitions to the archbishop of Paris. The prelate was moved by the Sister's revelations, and it was he who made a decision to have the medal struck. As an indication of his personal acceptance of the authenticity of the visions, the archbishop reserved the first medal for himself. So it was that the "Miraculous Medal" appeared in France for the first time in June of 1831, and in subsequent years many miracles were attributed to it. Through it, increased devotion to the Blessed Virgin spread to all corners of the globe.

What happened to Sister Catherine? How was her life affected by the visions? About six months before the Miraculous Medal came into existence, she was assigned to a hospice at Reuilly, not far from the motherhouse. There she labored for the elderly and the sick, devoting herself tirelessly to them for the remaining forty-six years of her life. She received no unusual attention or favors from the world or her order. On occasion it appears her superiors continued to think of her as an untutored peasant. She steadfastly kept the secret of the apparitions and her part in the inauguration of the medal. When the medals became available, she humbly received one along with the other members of her community and promised she would wear it with veneration. But the devotion to the Miraculous Medal needed promotion and an awareness of it among the faithful. The Daughters of Charity, along with the other order founded by St. Vincent de Paul (a group of priests known as Lazarists), undertook the task. As fast as the medals were produced, they were distributed all over France and beyond. It was called "the Medal that cures," "Mary's Medal," or "the Medal of the Immaculate Conception." Authenticated cures came swiftly. Two examples will suffice: A child seriously ill with cholera was given a medal and in a matter of minutes was cured; a young boy who had never been able to walk did just that after his mother started a novena to the Blessed Virgin.

At the hospice, Catherine was the cook and did other duties when necessary to assist the elderly residents. Her mystical experiences continued, and she is reported to have made some remarkable prophecies. She is reported as well to have had visions of the Cross. As she advanced in years, Catherine also became concerned that another request made to her by Our Lady was not being fulfilled — an altar to commemorate the second chapel apparition. It was to have a statue of the image of Mary that had appeared there.

Catherine had told her first confessor and, when he had died, his successor. Despite all her efforts, no action was ever taken; so the distraught nun, now aged seventy, decided to reveal to her superior that she was the Sister of the apparitions. The superior was humbled in her presence and regretted that she had treated Catherine as a nonentity within the community. She immediately agreed the work should be done, and a sculptor was commissioned to cast the statue, using the only witness who knew the details. It was now 1876, and Catherine was in very poor health. She did not live to see the fulfillment of Our Lady's request. She died on December 31, 1876.

When her death was announced, it was also revealed that it was to this simple Sister of Charity that Our Lady had appeared, and it seemed most of Paris wanted to honor her. For several years prior to her death, there had been rumors that she might be the visionary who had seen and conversed with the Blessed Virgin, but no one had known for sure. Now, as people passed the bier, they noticed the wrinkles of age had disappeared. She looked like a beautiful young woman again. The Daughters of Charity did not bury her in the community cemetery. Rather they found an unused vault in the chapel of the hospice and placed her there.

The cause for her canonization was not started until 1895. She was beatified on May 28, 1933, by Pope Pius XI, and canonized on July 27, 1947, by Pope Pius XII. An interesting note is that shortly before her beatification, St. Catherine's body was moved back to the chapel of the motherhouse. It was found to be incorrupt. She lies there now, amid the reality of the visions that took place while she humbly struggled to confirm her vocation as a handmaid of Jesus and Mary.

The Shrine of the Miraculous Medal at 140 Rue du Bac is not included in the ordinary tours of the French capital. Nevertheless, it is far from neglected; numerous travel agencies include it in organized pilgrimages to the shrines of Europe. The itinerary will allow about three days in Paris and then the pilgrims move on to Lourdes, Rome, or Fátima. But Paris is a fascinating place, and there are many religious shrines within its city limits or nearby. So a ten-day trip to the premier city of France can be absorbing and exciting.

Apart from the Miraculous Medal shrine, there is the Cathedral of Notre Dame, a Gothic miracle dating back to 1163, when construction on it began. From its towers one can see the whole city, and the climb toward the heavens is not merely a physical but also a spiritual experience. The interior of Notre

Dame is one of grandeur. Its magnificent windows contain some of the finest stained glass ever produced. Most impressive are three rose windows with glass dating back to about 1260, a decade after the completion of the cathedral.

Other churches of note are Saint-Sulpice and Saint-Germain-des-Prés. There are many others that can be found in the guidebooks and worthy of a visit. So too are the citadels of French culture such as the University of Paris, with its centerpiece, the Sorbonne. The Louvre, which probably houses the greatest art collection to be seen anywhere, will be one of the highlights of your visit. Even if you were to confine your time at the Louvre to viewing the Christian art of the masters, there would never be enough time to absorb it all.

Travel to France is easy from the U.S. There are nonstop flights from the East Coast, from the Midwest, and from the West Coast. No visas are required, and customs procedures are simpler than in many American airline terminals. Unless one is going on a pilgrimage or tour to other countries on the same trip, this is one time to be with a small group of friends or family. There are hotels and *pensions de famille* to fit almost every pocketbook, although one should stick to the central parts of Paris. It's easier to branch out from there to the various sites of interest.

Paris is a city for strolling, whether along its broad impressive boulevards or the lovely banks of the Seine. Walking instead of taking buses or taxis can be exhausting but at the same time exhilarating.

It's worth the effort, for one misses almost nothing of interest. Of course, a break from the city might be in order, and there are plenty of guided tours to such not-too-far attractions as the Cathedral of Chartres or the Palace of Versailles. Such tour information is available from hotels or the numerous tourist bureaus throughout the city.

We started out on the story of St. Catherine Labouré and the Shrine of the Miraculous Medal. But they are only part of the religious and spiritual history of Paris and France in general. That soil is rich in the glorious lives of saints as well as sinners. Suffering through centuries of war, plague, and revolution has not impaired the spiritual heritage of a country which produced Catherine Labouré, St. Vincent de Paul, St. Bernadette of Lourdes, and the Little Flower, St. Thérèse of Lisieux. There are many more in that history, sung and unsung, who gave authentic witness, which is our inspiration today.

MEDITATION

"Blessed are the pure in heart, for they shall see God" (Matthew 5:8). The country girl, simple and unlettered, who entered the convent of the Daughters of Charity, loved God with a pure heart. She gave her long life to him, taking care of the elderly, loving them as God loved her. She saw God in the holy sacrament of the altar, and she conversed with his Blessed Mother. But she also saw God in those cantankerous old men in her care. That is one way that God blesses "the pure in heart."

The medal for which she is responsible has been the source of greater love and devotion to Mary. It is an object so familiar that one sees it worn by Catholics on every continent. Like the rosary, it leads us through Mary to Jesus and blesses lives every day. To be able to visit the chapel where the Blessed Mother requested its use, is a moving experience and one to be cherished; but the message of the Miraculous Medal isn't limited to one geographical place. To become aware of the life of devotion to others, to the needy, to the elderly, that St. Catherine lived, is to see possibilities in our own lives for giving. The beatitudes were not intended only to bless a few, they were meant for me and you too. If we set about to live our lives with a pure heart, seeking no gratifications in power and prestige, we too will see God in those around us, those whom God chose to be part of our lives. We might even, indeed, have power and prestige but nonetheless with a pure heart refuse to let these influences rule us; then the joy that the sixth beatitude promises will be ours.

CHAPTER EIGHT

Our Lady of Fátima

Compared to the other shrines of Europe, Fátima is a relative newcomer. On a continent that is remarkable for shrines established a thousand or more years, the Fátima apparitions all took place just about seventy years ago, in 1917; yet the Church moved quickly to authenticate them — they were declared worthy of belief in 1930. And once again there is the same pattern: the Blessed Virgin appearing before humble peasant children, making prophecies, and urging prayer and penance for world peace.

Fátima lies about twenty-five miles inland and about seventy miles north-northeast of Lisbon, the capital of Portugal. This is a wild, rocky area of the country where peasants toil on hard, inhospitable land and where sheep roam the many foothills. In 1917, World War I was at its height and most of Europe was suffering from the carnage. In the village of Aljustrel, near Fátima, lived the dos Santos family, Antonio, Maria Rosa, and their seven children. The youngest member of this sturdy peasant family was nine-year-old Lucia. She was one of the visionaries, along with her two cousins, Francisco and Jacinta Marto, aged eight and six respectively.

It is said that Lucia already had had visions of angels, but, as a young child, she confided that to no one. The three children were close in age and interests. They were companions to one another, par-

Basilica of Our Lady of Fátima

ticularly during the days when they were responsible for the lonely chore of tending the sheep. It was while they were in the solitude of the hills accompanied only by the herd under their care that a vision came to them. It had started to rain heavily, and they ran to a cave seeking its protection against the storm. Suddenly, and without warning, they saw standing there before them a young man who told the children he was "the Angel of Peace." He taught them a prayer before he vanished as quietly as he had come. They saw him again twice that year (1916) and the experience changed their lives. By their own account they became centered on God, praying, fasting, and making reparation for the sins of the world. They did not want to draw attention to themselves nor appear different in any way, so outwardly they lived life as they were expected to. As a result, no one, not even their parents, knew of their experience and their new focus in life.

A day was to come when the events in the three youngsters' lives were no longer private but became extremely public. On that day, May 13, 1917, not only the children but the Church was eventually and deeply affected by the events which occurred. On that day, no angel messenger came; instead the Blessed Virgin herself appeared to the children.

The three were taking the sheep as usual to the family grazing ground when Mary appeared above a bush as "a Lady in white." She told them she was from heaven; that she wanted them to meet on this same day — the thirteenth — every month for six months and she would then reveal who she was. She also told them to say the Rosary for world peace and for the end of the war. While Francisco was present, he could not hear, so the others told him what the Lady had said. Then the children returned home, vowing to keep the vision secret. But the secret came out. The Marto children revealed it to their parents, who ridiculed them. Lucia suffered the same fate from her parents. The story got around as a bit of gossip, and eventually the whole village was laughing about the incident. June 13, the date for the next rendevous with the "Lady in white," came, and the three children — despite the jests and laughter — would not be deterred from the promised meeting. Accompanied by a tiny band of villagers, the three small believers arrived for the meeting at the appointed time. True to her word, and just as the children had reported, the Lady appeared again. This time she asked the children to recite the Rosary each day and told them to return to the same spot the following month. All three had a vision of the Immaculate Heart, and then the Lady went back up into the sky.

The July apparition was much the same as before, but there was one additional event — the Lady showed them the fires of hell and forecast more terrible wars if God was not obeyed. She also asked that Russia be consecrated to her Immaculate Heart and that first Saturdays of the month be reserved for reparation by receiving Holy Communion. The crowd of one thousand that had gathered believed this apparition was something special, and soon all Portugal knew about it. The story captured the hearts of the people, and soon the first pilgrimage to the apparition site at Cova da Iria took place. The children's parents were not happy with the events nor with the crowds that came and trampled all over their properties. During this period, Portugal was a republic with very anticlerical rulers hostile to religion. The country's leaders heard of the visions, and their local prefect at Ourem seized the children on August 13, the day they were supposed to see the Virgin. The children were subjected to interrogation and threats for two days before being released. But the Lady did appear to the children in nearby Valinhos on August 19, promising them a great miracle in October.

On September 13, a crowd of almost thirty thousand had gathered at the Cova da Iria, making it difficult for the children to get through. The Virgin appeared and urged the children to continue saying the Rosary to bring about the end of the war. She also promised that the next month they would see Our Lord, Our Lady of Mount Carmel, St. Joseph with the child Jesus, and Our Lady of Sorrows. Before she disappeared, she promised cures for some of the crowd who had asked for healing.

October 13 arrived, a wet and dreary day. Still, more than fifty thousand people were in attendance. Then the Virgin appeared and declared herself Our Lady of the Rosary. She pleaded for men and women to make amendments in their lives and do penance for sins. It was then that the sun came out of the clouds and shone brightly. It appeared to tremble, rotate violently, and fall over the heads of the onlookers before returning to the sky. Many in the crowd attested to seeing the "Miracle of the Sun." Even a prominent Lisbon journalist who had mocked the previous reports of the apparitions changed completely when reporting on this final apparition.

The Church in Portugal had kept a watch on the events taking place. An aide to the patriarch of Lisbon frequently conversed with the three visionaries. In 1922, a canonical process was inaugurated examining the apparitions. It lasted over seven years but led to the declaration by the bishop of Leiria, the diocese for Fátima, that the 1917 visions were authentic; at the same time he authorized the cult of Our Lady of Fátima.

Meanwhile, Lucia's two cousins, Francisco and Jacinta, had died: he of pneumonia on April 4, 1919, and his sister of pleurisy on February 20, 1920. This fulfilled the June 13 prophecy, when the Virgin told Lucia that she would soon take Francisco and Jacinta with her to heaven. Lucia was to remain to promote devotion to the Immaculate Heart. Lucia later became a Dorothean lay Sister at the convent in Tuy, Spain, and while there wrote down her remembrances of the apparitions in documents dated 1936, 1937, 1941, and 1942. The last document revealed the third section of the purported "Secret of Fátima," which was meant only for the reigning pope. The two other parts referred to the vision of hell and Our Lady's request for global devotion to her Immaculate Heart.

Lucia eventually joined the Carmelites at Coimbra, taking the religious name of Sister Mary of the Immaculate Heart.

The happenings at Cova da Iria in 1917 draw a million people each year to the Fátima shrine. Fátima (the name is Arabic in origin, reflecting the nine centuries of Islamic influence in the region) remains a solitary village. The popularity of the shrine is due largely to the known number of miraculous healings that have taken place since 1917. Many such cures have been carefully authenticated.

The people of Portugal have always had a special devotion to the Blessed Virgin. Almost every girl has Maria as at least part of her name, and in endless ways Mary is remembered continually by most believers. It is understandable then that the devotion to Our Lady of Fátima has led to an intense personal spiritual renewal among many of the faithful, and whole communities have attested to increased faith commitment.

In the late 1940s, a huge basilica was built; it houses the graves of Francisco and Jacinta Marto, whose beatification is being sought. When Pope Paul VI attended the Golden Jubilee celebrations on May 13, 1967, over one million people gathered in the huge square before the shrine and offered prayers for world peace. The future Pope John XXIII visited the Chapel of the Apparitions while he was still the patriarch of Venice. In the chapel is a beautiful statue of Our Lady of Fátima, made possible by donations from ordinary people from all around the world.

In the center of the vast esplanade in front of the basilica stands a huge monument to the Sacred Heart. It is used as the meeting place for pilgrimage groups and families. The square is surrounded by white marble columns that connect with retreat houses and the shrine hospital. From an architectural point of view, the basilica is not that impressive; but its two-hundred-foot tower is surmounted by a seven-ton bronze crown with a crystal cross. When lighted, the exterior of the basilica appears like a beacon for the whole countryside.

Perhaps one thing mars the area of the shrine — the sight of endless shops with vendors selling rosaries, statues, prayer books, and the like. The trouble is that some of the merchandise is of poor quality and of high price. Of course, the shop owners must make a living like the rest of us. However, it would probably be in the best interests of the pilgrims if the shops were farther away from the shrine.

How does one get to Fátima? From the U.S. there are direct flights to Lisbon. From other European cities there are frequent flights. With Lisbon being only an hour and a half away by road, going by bus or automobile is the quickest and easiest way to get to Fátima. The beaches of Portugal are clean and unpolluted, so you would enjoy the coastal road, which is excellent and which goes through some wonderful seaside villages and towns. One place worth stopping at is Nazaré, a small fishing village where you can see the fishermen bring in the afternoon catch and watch their families unload the boats. For several years, on the stone promenade above the beach, there stood a patriarchal figure with a long white beard who would invite tourists to have their picture taken with him. He made a living out of it, and his fee or honorarium was always negotiable. He may be standing there yet, awaiting your arrival.

There are more than sufficient hotels in Fátima and the surrounding towns. At the shrine too, there are a number of religious guesthouses. The Blue Army of Fátima, which is headquartered in the U.S., also has a guesthouse, normally with an American resident priest. Most of the available restaurants serve reasonably good food, and a few are quite excellent.

Inasmuch as Lisbon is relatively close, pilgrims or tourists may decide to stay there and make day visits to the shrine. There are also numerous other religious and historic attractions in the area and throughout Portugal. In Lisbon, one of the attractions is the Church of Madre de Deus, which is located near the docks. It is a magnificent church and was built by Queen Leonor in the sixteenth century. It houses the relics of one of the "Eleven Thousand Virgins of Cologne" and is well known for its priceless paintings, the beautiful carved woods, and gilded columns. There are many more exciting places to see in the Portuguese capital, and day tours from hotels and bus stations are available.

As this country borders on Spain, there are good roads into Portugal from Madrid and other major Spanish cities. If time permits, one scenic route from

Spain to Fátima is from La Coruña in Galicia, taking the coastal road to the Portuguese town of Viana do Castelo and on down to Leiria, then about ten miles or so southeast to Fátima. Whatever route you take, there will be places you won't want to miss.

Pilgrimages to Fátima are offered by a number of religious travel offices in the U.S. They can be directly to a particular shrine or as part of a package that includes other shrines in Europe. Always make sure that the travel agency has a good rating with the local Better Business Bureau or Chamber of Commerce. Check out the airline being used — some charter companies have a habit of leaving people stranded, and the regular airlines won't honor their tickets. I am not suggesting that you must be always suspicious, but it does pay to be careful when handing over large sums of money for a trip or a pilgrimage. You should feel secure when going on pilgrimage; it therefore behooves you to let a good agent handle all the arrangements.

Fátima offers the pilgrim very friendly hospitality. It is geared to handle the largest of crowds. The main pilgrimage season is from May to October, and on the thirteenth of those months the highways of Portugal are jammed with pilgrims. They come in cars, buses, campers, wagons, and on foot. As they travel, they pray, singing hymns and doing penitential acts. Many times their parish clergy travel with them, and they become a spiritual community of pilgrims. Some try to emulate the penance of their ancestors. It's not unusual to see pilgrims in the square at Fátima suffering painfully as they make the last few hundred yards to Mary's shrine on their knees. That's real prayer, real penance.

MEDITATION

"Pray without ceasing." How can this be possible when we each have to get on with our lives and can't remain kneeling forever? The people of Portugal can teach us how to do it. Fátima, though the most prominent shrine, is truly only one of many that they revere. Special days — including days of pilgrimage and processions — are frequent on their calendar. Somehow, they make a place for them in their busy lives. Yet, they don't wait for special days or special places to turn their attention to God. They embroider symbols — the cross, or the name of Jesus, or his Blessed Mother — on ordinary household objects. Every time they use the article, it is another reminder, another prayer. The Portuguese are not solemn, dreary people — they are a joyous, talkative, friendly race, with minds lifted up to the glories of God and his constant miracles. They are aware of miracles in their daily lives and recognize that for a miracle, you first need prayer. The two always go together.

Fátima should lead all of us to prayer and repentance, but the Portuguese can especially show us that the Christian is a person of joy. The message of Fátima is that we must rededicate our lives to the Lord, but it doesn't demand that this be done with grim, unsmiling features. We can sing with the pilgrims, but the hymns need not be slow and solemn. We can walk together in procession, but it need not be with downcast eyes and unhappy looks.

Fátima and the Portuguese remind us that by living so close to God, remembering him in all of the day's little moments is not a painful experience but a joyous one. True, there is sorrow in everyone's life and it cannot be avoided. But let's not pretend that God wants us to be miserable. As Jesus told us: "Blessed are you who weep now, for you shall laugh" (Luke 6:21).

CHAPTER NINE

Częstochowa

One of the most famous of Marian shrines in Europe lies deep in the heart of communist Poland. It was there centuries before the present regime was imposed upon the people, and it will be there centuries after the communists have gone the way of all tyrannies. Our Lady of Częstochowa is called "the heart of the Polish nation." The shrine is a place of international pilgrimage, but to the Polish people it is the pulsing center of all their joys and sorrows, their hopes and aspirations.

What makes this shrine an important place of pilgrimage is not only its history but also its positive and productive influence on Polish Catholicism and Polish culture. It has as its focus an icon known as the Black Madonna of Częstochowa, which is housed at the city's Pauline Monastery of Jasna Gora. The painting shows a rather dark-featured and sorrowful Mother and Child gazing out on the Polish nation and the world.

According to legend, the painting is attributed to St. Luke, one of the evangelists of the Gospels, who was also an artist. The legend states that after the crucifixion of her Son, Mary went to live with St. John and brought along a tabletop that had been made by Jesus and Joseph for their home. St. Luke is said to have painted the picture on the tabletop, using Mary as the live model. The Jasna Gora icon is of

Shrine of the Black Madonna

limewood, covered by canvas on which the painting has been applied. It is about two and a half feet by three and a half feet. The dark features are attributed by some to the smoke of many candles constantly surrounding the icon.

The St. Luke legend asserts that St. Helen, mother of Emperor Constantine, discovered the painting in Jerusalem and took it back to Constantinople about A.D. 325, along with other relics. It remained in the Byzantine capital for the next five hundred years but eventually found its way to a part of what is now Poland. However, some experts believe the icon is probably of ninth-century Greek or Greek-Italian origin, and there are signs of thirteenth-century overpaintings. Whatever the origin, there are historical records of its part in Poland's history and destiny.

The Catholic roots of the Polish people go back to the late tenth century, when the ruler of the area married a Christian princess and adopted Catholicism for himself and his people. Some suggest the Black Madonna came to Poland through the princess's family, who somehow obtained it after its five-hundred-year sojourn in Constantinople. Whatever the facts, it is known that the icon became a political as well as a religious symbol in the fourteenth century. During the constant military struggles of that era, the Ukraine became part of an increasingly powerful Polish empire. After Casimir the Great died in 1370, he was succeeded by Louis of Hungary. This king, according to one story, made one of his nephews the ruler of the Ukraine. The poor nephew spent most of his time defending his territory against the Russians. He did well in battle and became the prince of Belsk, then a part of his fiefdom. It is recorded that one of his first official acts was to pray before a miraculous painting called the Black Madonna. When the Tartars attacked Belsk, one of their arrows entered the chapel and struck the icon, leaving a permanent scar in the throat of the Virgin. The prince was once again victorious but decided to remove the icon to his birthplace, a town named Opala. On the way, the prince and his entourage stopped overnight at Częstochowa. The icon was placed in a local church where the townspeople spent the night praying before it.

The story is told that the following morning the horses pulling the prince's wagon refused to budge, no matter what was done to persuade them. And the cart could not be moved when unhitched — even by the strongest men around. Then the prince told the crowd that he had had a dream in which an angel told him the Madonna was to stay in Częstochowa. The behavior of the horses and the fact that the wagon could not be moved, he said, convinced him that the dream was truly a message from God. The Black Madonna stayed and eventually, around 1382, was placed in the Jasna Gora monastery. The Polish nation honors August 26, 1382, as the day the icon was placed in that simple wooden church.

The fame of the miraculous Black Madonna spread rapidly, and the monastery grew and prospered through the number of pilgrims who came to pay homage to the Virgin. But fame also had its price — the monastery was frequently the target of large bands of robbers from nearby countries. In one such attempt, around 1430, it is said that the invaders were thwarted in their attempts to steal some monastery treasure and they vented their frustration on the icon. They are said to have cast it to the ground, jumped on it, and used horses to trample it. The icon was broken into several pieces, but the center part holding the face remained intact. The robbers slashed the face with their swords, leaving deep gashes in the right cheek of the painting. Unfortunately, the gashes could not be eradicated even in the expert restoration that took place later.

The ruler of Poland with whom the Black Madonna is most closely identified is Jadwiga, the youngest daughter of King Louis. In commemoration of her coronation, she asked the Blessed Virgin to take Poland under her protection. She later married Jagiello of Lithuania, who converted to the faith along with his whole nation. The original Jasna Gora church housing the shrine was built by King Jagiello after his coronation in 1386.

Three centuries later the area was fortified, enclosing a pilgrim city. In 1655, there was a siege of Częstochowa by antipope forces from Sweden. They were repulsed, and a year later Our Lady of Częstochowa was proclaimed "Queen of Poland," becoming the symbol of Polish national and religious liberty.

The next two centuries were hard times for Częstochowa. It was taken by the Russians in 1771, by the Prussians in 1793, and the French in 1806. It ceased to be a fortified city in 1813 when the Russian czar took the icon to be venerated in St. Petersburg, now known as Leningrad.

The present shrine church was built in 1644. The huge 344-foot-high tower, added in 1702, dominates the city. In 1717, Pope Clement XI authorized the crowning of the icon in his name in solemn ceremonies at the shrine. Nowadays, despite the restrictions placed on the people by the Polish regime, over a million pilgrims go to Jasna Gora each year. Some of them belong to the large Polish community in the U.S., where the Black Madonna of Częstochowa is revered with equal fervor.

Pope John Paul II, the first Pole and Slav to be elevated to the papacy, made a pilgrimage to Jasna Gora in 1979, shortly after he began his pontificate. He wanted to be present at the six hundredth anniversary of the arrival of Our Lady of Częstochowa, held in 1982, but it wasn't possible. Millions of Poles and others from all over the globe did attend and manifested an outpouring of faith seldom witnessed in any other part of the world.

Getting to Częstochowa from North America is not that difficult. The Polish airline LOT has direct flights from New York to Warsaw. Some U.S. as well as other European airlines can get you to Warsaw through London, Paris, Frankfort, Rome, and other places. There are adequate flights from Warsaw to

Częstochowa. On arrival in Poland, the usual options are open for onward travel. There is a good bus service, a good train service, and there is the rent-a-car option. Arrangements for the latter should be made through an agency in the U.S. because of the cheaper rate. One thing to keep in mind regarding automobiles: When traveling by car in Europe, you will find that gas prices are horrendous compared to those in the U.S. Also, in eastern Europe one has to be careful to stick to routes that have been approved. Foreigners are always looked upon with suspicion by the authorities in these countries. It's best to go by the rules and avoid trouble.

What we have said above applies mostly to individuals or families going on their own to Częstochowa. But unless you have relatives or good friends in Poland, it's better to go with a group tour or pilgrimage. Apart from the fact that it is always cheaper that way, it avoids a lot of hassles. Everything from transportation to accommodations to meals is taken care of. The only worry left is what to see and what gifts to buy — and the tour guides will assist in that.

Joining a tour group is best through an experienced travel agency, especially if you are going to eastern Europe. Most deal directly with the government tourism bureaus, arrange the group visas, generally know where the best accommodations are, the most interesting places to visit, and the most scenic ways to get there.

Częstochowa's main attraction is Jasna Gora and its Black Madonna icon. The city is like most eastern

European industrial centers — austere, drab, but clean. It has a population of about one hundred seventy-five thousand and many churches. The hotels are clean and comfortable, but don't expect too many American-style amenities: They don't exist. Then again, the purpose of the visit or pilgrimage is to see the Virgin's shrine, and a penitential approach accepts the possibility of mixing austerity with joy.

MEDITATION

The history of the icon of Our Lady of Częstochowa shows us, like a beacon in the darkness, that God is with us in times of trial and tribulation, joy and gladness. Over the centuries we can follow the Polish nation's path and discover God supporting and giving strength to individuals and the nation as a whole. The words of the Twenty-third Psalm seem appropriate as we meditate on the meaning of Częstochowa: "... He restores my soul. / He leads me in paths of righteousness. . . . / Even though I walk through the valley of the shadow of death, / I fear no evil; / for thou art with me. . ." (vv. 3-4).

Today's domination by atheistic communists and their efforts to eliminate religion are not the first persecution the Polish people have had to endure. They confidently know they will keep the faith until that wonderful day finally arrives and communism has been overcome. The unifying force that is both the blessing and the miracle of Częstochowa has created in leaders and ordinary people the courage to defy their overlords. The example of the faith-filled and fearless children who successfully protested against the removal of crucifixes from classrooms shows how the national devotion produces individual heroes.

The shrine to Our Lady leads all of us to her Son. Through her Son we can see opportunities to lead true Christian lives, whatever the external circumstances. In our human weaknesses we falter, and thus we fail to measure up when the strength to act or just to hang on is offered us through prayer. Prayer at Częstochowa is unceasing. The result of those prayers is frequently found in our daily paper when we read of yet another instance of the Polish people showing the world that Christ and his Blessed Mother are ever present in the lives of the people of Poland.

CHAPTER TEN

St. Meinrad of Einsiedeln

The ancient Swiss place of pilgrimage — St. Meinrad of Einsiedeln — has much in common with other shrines in Europe. There, a martyred saint is honored; there, a "Black Madonna" is revered; and there, pilgrims go to be healed spiritually and physically. Einsiedeln is situated in the scenic countryside about an hour outside Zurich; it includes a Benedictine monastery whose foundation roots go back to the early tenth century. Within the abbey is the shrine containing a statue of Our Lady, darkened with age and given the name which describes its appearance. It is now partially restored in bright red and gold colors, with only the face and hands untouched. Again, the colors of the Black Madonna come from the centuries it has stood there combined with the smoke of the millions of candles that have been lighted before it.

The shrine was built to honor St. Meinrad, who was born near Württemberg, Germany, in the late eighth century. He was educated at Reichenau Abbey, where he became a Benedictine monk and priest. Later he was headmaster of a school on upper Lake Zurich and subsequently left the world to become a hermit. He set up his hermitage on the slopes of Mount Etzel around 828 and eventually built a chapel which later became the site for the future Einsiedeln monastery. Meinrad spent his days

Abbey of Einsiedeln

praying and fasting and working in the fields to provide for his daily food. His reputation as a holy hermit was known to the populace all around. Taking to heart the belief that hospitality was one of the marks of a true Christian, Meinrad did not use the fact that he was a hermit to excuse himself from this obligation. On January 21, 861, he was slain by two robbers to whom he had given food and friendship. There is a legend told that like St. Francis of Assisi, this saint was close to nature and nature's creatures. Some ravens who were Meinrad's friends witnessed the killing and made such a noise as they followed the robbers that the townspeople apprehended them and brought them to justice.

Meinrad was buried in his home abbey of Reichenau, but his body was taken back to Einsiedeln in 1039. The symbol of St. Meinrad is two ravens, the birds who helped bring his murderers to justice. Einsiedeln remains today a Benedictine abbey. It has further status as a Benedictine abbey with an abbot nullius, which means it has ecclesiastical jurisdiction over some parishes and institutions normally reserved to a diocese. In addition, the abbot of Einsiedeln ranks with the bishops of the bishops' conference in Switzerland. Dedicated to Our Lady of the Hermits, the abbey is located in the diocese of Chur in central Switzerland. Founded in 934, it had as its first abbot a monk named Eberhart who ruled twenty-four years. The abbey was favored by local royalty; it was granted immunity, and the abbot was made a prince of the empire. Between 1029 and 1577 the abbey was destroyed by fire five times. In addition, there were other problems such as the restriction of novices to the nobility. At one point in history, this limited the monks to fewer than five. After 1350, the liturgy as well as the care of pilgrims was given over to secular priests. Zwingli, who later on would be one of the Swiss leaders of the Reformation, served as pastor at Einsiedeln from 1516 to 1518. During all this time of turmoil, pilgrims still flocked to the shrine from all parts of Europe. In fact, it was not unusual for fifty thousand persons to visit the Black Madonna within the space of one week. It has had continuity, but radical changes have occurred. In the middle of the sixteenth century, reforms were introduced at Einsiedeln, and fifty years later the Swiss Benedictine Congregation was founded. Printing was introduced into the abbey in 1664, and once again the abbots elected were devoid of politics and chosen for their scholarship and spiritual leadership.

During a particularly turbulent period in Europe, French troops sacked the abbey and destroyed the church in 1798. Three years later, the monks returned to rebuild. The main monastery building dates back to 1718; but the church, consecrated in 1735, has been restored several times, the latest restoration being completed in 1943.

The shrine of Our Lady is the focal point of everything that takes place in Einsiedeln. It is there that the statue of the Black Madonna is venerated by thousands of pilgrims each year. Legends concerning the origin of the statue abound, but the one most accepted is that it was given to St. Meinrad around 850 by Hildegard, abbess of Zurich. Whatever may be the accuracy of these legends, it has prompted joy, healing, spiritual renewal, faith, and fervor among countless supplicants over the ages who have visited this area of rolling hills and endless woods.

The approaches to the baroque monastery are somewhat marred by the commercialization that seems to have taken over some aspects of the holy ground. All kinds of small shops form a semicircle in front of the entrance. It gives one the sense of "buy now, pray later." Still, it should not deter pilgrims from heading for the beautiful fountain of the Madonna, where they can enjoy its healing waters. Legend says that this is a well made holy because Jesus visited the place, drank from its water, and blessed it.

In the center of the building, at the top of the façade, stands a magnificent statue of St. Meinrad, with two domed towers standing sentry at either side. It is as if the martyred Benedictine saint is daring the world to come to this quiet country place and accept the only peace possible — the peace of the Lord.

Soon after entering the abbey, one comes across the celebrated shrine to Mary. Again, legend plays a major part in the tradition, backed up by strong faith. It is said that Christ commanded his angels to consecrate the shrine. For that reason, it is said, the Black Madonna has survived all the wars and upheavals of the past eleven centuries.

How to get to Einsiedeln? There is of course good air service to Zurich from the United States and from every major European capital. Once you're there, all the options of further travel are available. There is a first-rate rail service, with several trains a day. There are buses and — as always — rent-a-car.

Switzerland is an excellent place to take a family, and the scenery is unmatched in any other part of Europe. The visit to Einsiedeln can be part of a general tour of Europe or just confined to Switzerland, with stops in Geneva, Lucerne, Bern, Zurich, and Fribourg. In all these cities there are many places of both religious and historical significance.

Whether you are on a tight budget or able to spend freely, there are adequate accommodations available, from luxury hotels to bed and breakfast in private homes. It's always good to check for the latter with the local tourist information bureau. We always repeat that making the rent-a-car reservation in the U.S. can save money; however, as mentioned before, don't expect fuel to be anything but expensive — in fact, startling to Americans.

Einsiedeln does offer accommodations in local hotels, and some of the village restaurants are quite good. It is probably a good place to stay if you are making an individual or family pilgrimage and are not rushing to get to another place. That's the major drawback in going on group pilgrimages. Everything is normally arranged perfectly. The pilgrim doesn't have to worry about anything but personal chores. To accomplish this pilgrimage, sponsors try to crowd in a great deal. For example, a two-week tour of European shrines can involve six to eight places. This means spending only a day or a day and a half in each place. That's not adequate for places like Einsiedeln — especially if you wish also to make it a kind of spiritual retreat. It is understood that the budget-conscious pilgrim will have to put up with all the rushing around that a group tour plan usually entails. But for those who can afford the cost and time, it's worthwhile to stay a bit longer for prayer.

One last interesting note about Einsiedeln: From this Swiss abbey emerged St. Meinrad's Abbey in St. Meinrad, Indiana. This is the oldest monastery in the Swiss-American Benedictine Congregation and was established as a priory in 1854. It became an abbey in 1870 and has contributed much to the priestly and religious-education life of this country. Catholics throughout the country are familiar with Abbey Press, and every parish seems to have someone who studied at St. Meinrad's in Indiana. It has been an effective influence on American Catholic life.

MEDITATION

"A sower went out to sow his seed; . . ." (Luke 8:5) — this introduction to the Parable of the Sower is well known to all of us. There, in Einsiedeln — a tiny corner in a tiny country — the seeds of prayer, faith, and love of God were sown centuries ago. A few of the seeds fell on hard ground and dissension and trouble developed. A few of the seeds were weeds that produced leaders who were politically able but spiritually impoverished. Eventually these wayward seeds died away, but the good seeds flourished. From the good seeds came lives devoted solely to the glory of God and love for one's fellowman. The abbey is a model of servanthood where the self is not a priority.

As we meditate on the ability of the Benedictines to reform and revitalize, we can see a similar thread in our own lives. How often have we become aware of our own failure to act according to our belief, to live as we profess we believe? How often have we made an effort to reform and revitalize ourselves? It's part of the whole human story, the realization that we are not living up to our noblest ideals and the determination to regain what we have lost. It happens to institutions and it happens in personal lives. What truly matters is that we thank God for opening our eyes to what is wrong and for giving us the strength to do something about it. No matter what the root of the problem may be, or how many times before we have tried to make it right, we'll try again. We know that we will succeed when we give it to God and use his strength instead of relying on our own, "For with God nothing will be impossible" (Luke 1:37). In the words of Jesus himself, "What is impossible with men is possible with God" (Luke 18:27).

In the history of Einsiedeln we have a perfect example of an institution which changed because nothing is impossible with God. We know the words of Jesus can apply to our lives too, and even what seems impossible today can one day be a blessed reality.